For Those Who Dream of Crushing Dreams

So You Want To Be A Dictator

A Supreme Leadership Guide for the Aspiring Authoritarian

C. T. Jackson

Contents

Welcome, Future Oppressor

"If this were a dictatorship, it would be a heck of a lot easier... as long as I'm the dictator. Hehehe."

— George W. Bush, Painter

It is no secret that much of humanity is dumb. Look at the last few years; people are really, really dumb. If you do not believe that you may want to stop here, assuming you were able to read this far. If not, don't worry, there are pictures for you to look at. A hundred thousand years of evolution isn't much time to improve on what is essentially still a reptilian chunk of neurons in the grand scheme of things. Humans have tamed fire, pushed out into space, and created the chalupa, but these are mere highlights in a history of a species that has drunkenly stumbled through its short time in existence.

Elected government has been a mostly ineffective method of managing humanity – the smart, the mediocre, and the tragically ignorant. Some versions of governance have worked in the past, and some even work now. In recent times, there has been a dramatic shift toward the need for total control over an increasingly misinformed population.

So there has been a shift toward authoritarianism, or dictatorship. According to Stalin's Dictionary, authoritarianism is defined as "A totally legitimate governing mechanism that never does any harm to anyone." According to more legitimate sources, it is defined simply as blind submission to a leader (or group of leaders) who will determine every aspect of their subjects' lives. Whether it is about what you are allowed to say, what you are allowed to own, who you should hate, or who you should love (answer: it's the dear leader), authoritarianism takes the burden of making choices away from the people. It promotes a simple life, one free of the complexities of the modern world.

Authoritarianism goes by many names: theocracy, dictatorship, military junta, homeowner's association (HOA), shogunate, caudillo, autocracy, despotism, PTA president, hedge fund CEO, tsarism, and Ellen DeGeneres. Each has unique characteristics that this book will explore, but all have one key similarity: absolute power.

This book is meant to serve as an easy-to-follow guide for aspiring dictators. As the collaborative governments of the world fall or fail outright, there is a need across the geopolitical landscape for iron-fisted overlords to keep the populace in line and placated. The global population continues to grow exponentially, but there is a clear lack of the amoral individuals required to handle it and keep it under control. Some progress has been made in the past couple of decades, but the future is calling for more control – and less control (depending on where your boot heel stands).

However, this book isn't just a half-assed history lesson. Don't worry, it will at least be half-assed. This book is for those who seek power, and who seek to oppress those who deserve it as well as those who don't deserve it. It is for those people who believe they know what is right for the rest of humanity, who need a hobby, who like uniformity, and who dream of unprincipled glory. In short, readers, this is for you. But who are you?

CAREER POLITICIANS

You are already in "the game" so you have a leg up in many of the areas required for grabbing hold of absolute power. Being in the system means you have additional avenues through which to streamline your path toward absolute power. Beware though; others are sure to see through your schemes as you move up the career politician ladder.

This guide will help you with the internal tactics to curry favor with the higher-ups, gain sycophants to carry you forward to glory, stomp out competitors, and backstab colleagues on your way to the top. In this game, party affiliation doesn't matter, whether it is Democrat, Republican, green, selfish libertarian, or whatever those odd European ones are. All that matters is power.

PARENTS

Why not build upon your tiny despotic kingdom? You already have a strong grip on the authoritarian strength that comes with being a parent. When kids ask why they have to eat vegetables, dress up for church, or see Grandma, all you have to say is "because I said so." That is a dictator's ultimate dream, and you are already living it. In addition, small children act similarly to the moronic, drunken citizens in your country. They will hang onto every word you say, and they will respond well to fear or punishment. You cannot send your children to the labor camps, but you can tell them you can. This guide can help you get to that reality. It can be scary becoming the parent of tens of millions of people, but at least child services won't be knocking on your door. This is mostly because you can disband the whole organization. Isn't parenting fun? Authoritarian parenting is even more fun. Corporal punishment is back!

IDEALISTS

Perhaps you just finished your Political Philosophy 101 class, maybe you have been spending more nights at your local community board meetings, or maybe you have a bunch of books on socialism that you've "read." You might even be the real deal; the key is that you have a "vision." And that vision can be corrupted or be used to justify anything you ever want to do. You have probably written down more than a few ideas on how a utopian government should be run – borrowing heavily from Plato and Aristotle no doubt, you fraud. Fraud is good though, so lean into that throughout your campaign toward absolute power.

Your ideas go beyond a philosophical debate at the local watering hole after a few whiskeys with your friends. The thought of being a benevolent dictator doesn't sound so far-fetched then. Well, this book will help you garner the respect, gain the support, and get your "original" thoughts onto a serviceable platform. From there, well, the sky is the limit. Out of Plato's Cave and into the streets – this book will get you there and then you can leave that pesky philosophy behind.

Retirees Looking for a New Hobby

For those of you lucky enough to have the finances to retire, good for you. You do not need to take a part-time greeting job at Walmart or slave in the salt mines of the upcoming hellscape future. This book will help you find a great way to pass the time in your twilight years.

No need to spend your pension money on stamp collecting or model ship kits. Why not utilize those hard-earned dollars on methods to further restrict those who have come and will come after you. It is not like the future generations will ever see any of those dollars, given their retirement plan is to die in the climate wars. Destroying the future of the youth doesn't have to stop when you retire. It just gets better with age.

Military Brass

Whether you have admirably served your country on the field of battle, or you simply wash down statues serving in the National

Guard, you have an easy route into leading a military junta. While these often work best outside of the industrialized world, the military boasts a fine reputation for the strength, manpower, and discipline needed to dismantle the civilian aspects of any government.

This book will help you with the tactics needed to quickly move up the hierarchy of the defense structure of any country. You can reach a point where you can intimidate the civilian population and parts of government. Or you can convince them to support your cause. Start practicing your strongman hand gestures and designing pointless medals to cover your chest.

TEACHERS

Every teacher who is reading this is probably nodding their head in agreement. Especially those that teach elementary school. As an elementary school teacher, you have to deal with naïve, basically intoxicated people running around like maniacs and shooting off their mouths all day. A strong arm and discipline are essential for controlling this tiny population. You have the quiet, calm group. You have the loud, obnoxious group. And you have the group that fits somewhere in the middle. You need to cater to all of them while ensuring you maintain a high level of order. The methods you use to punish these children and keep them in line will translate well into reigning over a larger, older population, albeit one that often maintains the same level of self-awareness and intelligence as toddlers.

CHILDREN OF ALL AGES

Lastly, who can forget about the children? They truly are our future, so you must stop them now before they get too powerful. However, this book doesn't discriminate, it just teaches discrimination. In case this author lives long enough, please remember how he helped you, future oppressor.

In the face of every smiling child, in every twinkle of their eye, there is a mass murdering egomaniac waiting to come out. This book will encourage the next generation of oppressors to flourish through lessons on indoctrination, judging others for petty reasons, psychological bullying, finding a passion and having it taken away, triggering a lifelong hatred of the world and a desire to exact revenge, and many other easy-to-do activities children can use to reach their potential while denying others theirs.

OVERVIEW OF THIS GUIDE

This guide is divided into three main sections. The first section provides a solemn overview of democracy. Just kidding; it's actually a celebration of the death of democracy. And a primer of authoritarianism and its roots. It provides context for the retreating trend of democracy and shows how authoritarianism is already beginning to fill the vacuum left behind. Finally, it discusses what it means to be a dictator, to help the reader understand the mindset of the maniacal.

The second section dives into the methods, activities, and tactics of becoming a dictator. This includes developing a platform (a shallow one to be sure), practicing the modus operandi of an authoritarian, and choosing what to wear as you build your dictatorial wardrobe. We will look at how to achieve, or steal power through such fun activities as demagoguery, intimidation, bribery, projection, and fraud.

The final section celebrates your victory as supreme leader. It aims to help you define the first months and years of your reign of terror. Victory is only the beginning, as this section helps you ensure your reign is everlasting, with tips on avoiding coups, quashing uprisings, and faking the democratic process to placate the masses. The appendix includes a helpful barometer for stacking up your achievements against those authoritarian pioneers who came before you.

This book is for all those who dare to dream of power,

oppression, and unbridled strength. It is for those who seek to better themselves and reach their career aspirations at the expense of everyone else. Welcome, future despot, and good luck on your journey to total domination.

Chapter 1

Rejoice! Democracy is Dead

"Remember, democracy never lasts long. It soon wastes, exhausts, and murders itself."

— John Adams, Star of the "John Adams" limited series on HBO

Since its inception, democracy has been much like a drunkard at the bar. With the first few drinks, it is cogent, its ideas make sense, and they are well received by the rest of the patrons. However, as time goes on, and it sucks down more gin and tonics, it gets more incoherent and angrier. Eventually, it either falls asleep in the street or attempts to fight those around it, with no one winning in the end. As dawn peeks through the clouds, and the booze begins to wear off, those still around realize how pathetic and embarrassing democracy was last night. The people decide to move on for good, and democracy decides it never needed them in the first place. It eventually overdoses on a combination of its own pride and fentanyl. Good riddance.

Before we get into the festivities about the death of the people's moronic rule, let's look back at democracy and its time in the sun. Yes, it is time for a history lesson. Don't worry, there won't be any academia or citations[1] here, just sit back and relax. Before you continue, please cue up Sarah McLachlan's, "I Will Remember You" on your media device, assuming it is a state-approved one.

ANCIENT DEMOCRACY – A FOOL'S DISCOVERY

508 BC is often considered the theoretical birth of democracy. The wheelbarrow was invented around the same time, but it remains far more useful today. The Greeks managed to front-load their contributions to the world by developing democracy and then doing not much else for the next 2,500 years. The concept originated in Athens, back when the Greeks made much better economic and political decisions. The Athenians utilized this early form of democracy to pass legislation as well as for the executive branch for passing additional bills for the state. The idea of democracy was based on property ownership, with a class structure supported by the number of bushels of grain a person owned. The lowest class was comprised of laborers who could not hold office and did not hold property – much like today. Time is a flat circle. Let's face it, a 2,500-year life ain't bad for a form of government.

After 200 years, the democratic experiment ended after the death of Alexander the Great. The Roman Empire would pick up pieces for a few decades before having a Caesarean to remove the democratic government and allow it be adopted by others.

MODERN DEMOCRACY – THE WASTED CENTURIES

Modern democracy first became more permanently established in the early 18th century with the first Parliament of Great Britain, following the merger of England and Scotland, a union that would never encounter any issues again.

Parliaments continued to be formed in other countries around the world, but it wasn't until the late 18th century that the ball really got rolling. Of course, this was due to the American

Revolution. Given that America is the center of the universe, this was the peak for democracy until World War II.

Americans managed to compose a number of beautiful documents to showcase the power of democracy. The most famous of these is *Hamilton*, the musical. The others, like the Bill of Rights, Declaration of Independence, the Constitution, and *Rocky IV* helped changed the direction of democracy for the next several decades.

Just a few years later, France decided to make a nice lunch of baguettes and bags of heads. In 1789, the poor masses stormed the Bastille and launched the French Revolution. (A bunch of American idiots would try to use a similar tactic over two centuries later.) King Louis XVI was facing an economic crisis and tried to raise taxes (not on the rich though, that would be insane!). The people thought that Louis had lost his head, given his outrageous demands. So they made it a reality, along with nearly 10,000 others. A man named Robespierre would seek out any critics to the revolution and relieve them of their heads. He would end up being deemed too harsh and be guillotined as well. You should be taking notes. You don't want to end up with an angry crowd at your palace gates, particularly a French one.

In the mid-20th century, the United States single-handedly won World War II without any help from anyone. Following this win, democracy became the dominant form of government across the world, even though the pesky Soviets tried to push their beliefs onto the world during the post-war years.

Over the next few decades, democracy attempted a comeback tour. It found temporary footholds in Portugal, Greece (back again for more), and many of the Eastern European countries as the Soviet Union collapsed. However, much like most musicians' comeback tours, it was not well received.

It wasn't until the 1980s that democracy started to become a burden on the various peoples of the world. Or at least it wasn't until then that people began to truly realize how much of a burden voting was and always had been.

By the early 2000s, the idea of democracy was looked at with more disdain than approval, as people realized that their clueless neighbors had the same amount of power (when measured in votes) as they did. The first decades of the new millennia continued to see an exponential backsliding of democracy, also known as autocratization (see, you will learn something in this book!). The weakening of political institutions is the main harbinger of democracy's death knell. For instance, a legislature that cannot pass any laws, cooperate, and seems mostly corrupt and inept (sound familiar?) is one that is just asking to be overthrown. Increasing polarization between parties, religions, ethnicities, and the question of whether Lebron James or Michael Jordan is the best NBA player further degraded democracy. One of the final nails in the coffin was the erosion of the free and fair press. A desire to monopolize and constantly entertain the masses left little room for actual information and educated discussion. By 2015, the anger of the bored and moronic masses had overwhelmed the intelligentsia across global democracies.

Aspiring dictators around the globe attempted to harness this anger. Many of them succeeded in winning their elections and taking complete control. There were – and still are – countries that haven't yet given up; but as of the start of the new decade, democracy is in hospice. All that is left is to put your pillow over its face and hold it there. Shhh, democracy, it is OK. They can't hurt you anymore. Go to sleep, forever.

FUNERAL FOR AN ENEMY

Fig. 1: Don't Cry Because Democracy Is Over, Cry Because It Happened

As we lower the mangled body of democracy into the ground,

let us not fret, but rejoice, for a new era has dawned. An era ruled by you dear reader – and soon to be dear leader. Citing recent statistics from Freedom House (one of the few legitimate statistics this book will cite, because, well, you know how we feel about legitimacy), democracy has declined at an accelerated pace in every region of the world, with fewer than 20 percent of people living in fully free countries. So, my wannabe oppressors, the world truly is yours for the taking. And dictatorship does offer substantial travel benefits.

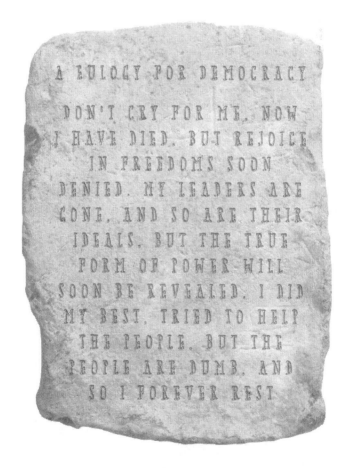

A EULOGY FOR DEMOCRACY

DON'T CRY FOR ME, NOW I HAVE DIED. BUT REJOICE IN FREEDOMS SOON DENIED. MY LEADERS ARE GONE, AND SO ARE THEIR IDEALS. BUT THE TRUE FORM OF POWER WILL SOON BE REVEALED. I DID MY BEST, TRIED TO HELP THE PEOPLE. BUT THE PEOPLE ARE DUMB, AND SO I FOREVER REST

Before you pick out your country to rule, you may want to take a sabbatical to visit some of your eventual dictatorial peers and see how well they are ruling their despotic kingdoms. Let's look at this year's top destinations for the traveling, future dictator. What failed state is on your bucket list?

BELARUS

Alexander Lukashenko welcomes you to his post-Soviet paradise, still very much in the satellite oversight of Vladimir Putin – it even still has its own KGB. Lukashenko has been in power since 1994, when the office of president was created. He has had a pretty impressive reign given that he is the only president in the current history of Belarus. Lukashenko refers to himself as "Europe's last dictator," and has worked his darndest to earn that title. In 2020, he violently persecuted protestors accusing him of rigging the election (spoiler: he did). His most notable recent accomplishment has been forcing a Ryanair (i.e., The Bus of the Skies) flight carrying a prominent dissident to land in the Belarusian capital so he could be arrested. Since 1994, Belarus has kept up a rich history of torture, sexual abuse, assassination plans on dissidents abroad, and state-sponsored terrorism.

AZERBAIJAN

Welcome to the nepotistic wonderland of Azerbaijan! Ilham Aliyev is happy to have your company, despite him not smiling in any picture ever. Enjoy the food, the dry desert heat, and the exorbitant number of human rights violations, including torture, arbitrary arrests of dissidents (or just people Aliyev doesn't like) and harassment of journalists. Do you need to launder some funds for your push to authoritarian rule? Azerbaijan will be happy to help as the Aliyev family is well versed in money-laundering for various European politicians. They even tried to help Mr. Donald Trump build one of his hideous towers here. There is plenty to learn here and Mr. Aliyev hopes you enjoy the company of Corruption Magazine's 2012 "Person of the Year."

Venezuela

Bienvenidos! The dishonorable Nicolas Maduro welcomes you to his South American utopia. Put your feet up and relax in his villa as he attempts to maintain power through the extensive oil reserves that Venezuela exports to the rest of the world. Maduro, who assumed power in 2013, has maintained a heavy hand on dissidents and issued a steady stream of rhetoric against the Western powers, utilizing a communist background to relate to the people. Enjoy the wonderful buffet spread as the majority of the country starves due to some of the most boneheaded economic policies ever developed in the modern world. Pack your swim trunks, but don't forget your body armor as crime and homicides have increased by over 20 percent.

Gondor

Alatulya, weary traveler. Welcome to Middle Earth. Lord Denethor II of the Westfold is happy to entertain you. He has ruled this kingdom for over 30 years, and if you call him Steward he will burn you with wood and oil. His kingdom is one of strength as they are in a continuous war with enemies all around. Denethor took power from the last king, and he will be damned if he ever gives it up to any rightful heir. Call it a passive coup. Even now, his paranoia is starting to make him believe you are trying to dethrone him. Did Gandalf send you? Denethor believes in sending soldiers to their death without a second thought and he will happily use them to keep the populace in line if they argue with his deranged rule. Please enjoy the White City, and may he interest you in some cherry tomatoes?

United States

Do you have a visa? If not, get the hell out. Unless you are white, in which case, welcome! Unfortunately, the country is currently suffering from a legitimately elected leader in Joe Biden. But rest assured, there is a large group of true believers ready to show you how to storm a capital. Hopefully you will be more successful.

Deposed leader and human orange, Donald Trump will be happy to welcome you to his home in Mar-A-Lago. Let him mouth off for a while but pay attention to his use of state-run television like Fox News, OANN, and HGTV. Do not be alarmed by the insane idiots of his MAGA tribe and QAnon. Instead, take notes on how you too can starve the education system for decades, hijack social media, and create a disheveled army of sycophants ready to serve your every whim. After all, when you are dictator you "Grab democracy by the p*ssy. When you are a despot they just let you do it." Nothing but class here in the good old US of A.

CHAPTER 2

A DESPOT'S TIME TO SHINE

"I don't care if they respect me, so long as they fear me."

— CALIGULA, FAMOUS EQUESTRIAN

Authoritarianism is not just a state of mind, but it certainly helps if you first overthrow the state. Let's take a brief look at the early pioneers of absolute power. These men – yes, they were all men, welcome to the historical patriarchy – paved the way toward authoritarianism through blood, often literally paving over human remains.

SULLA: THE ARTIST FORMERLY KNOWN AS STATESMAN

Sulla of Ancient Rome holds the distinction of reviving the Roman dictatorship by capitalizing on foreign wars. The office of dictator in the past had been one of duty, a need to control the empire during major crises. It was meant to be a temporary position, but one that served a useful purpose when decisions needed to be made quickly.

Once Sulla gained full control over the empire in 81 BC, he

instituted a series of programs that focused on executing enemies of the state, confiscating their property, and redistributing it among his loyalists and himself. These types of actions would be inherited by modern dictatorships and continue to be an important strategy that any new authoritarian must use in their early days of rule.

While he was the first official dictator, Sulla unfortunately returned his powers to the Republic and withdrew from public life (what a dolt). He focused on his memoirs and passed away due to chronic alcohol abuse; most scholars believe it was the inordinate number of Red Bull and vodkas. His mistake at ceding power would not thankfully be repeated often; future authoritarians learned that once you gain that level of power, you don't let go. Think of that old cat poster, "Hang In There Baby."

Caesar: Ides and Ideas

The eponymous salad does not do justice to what Julius Caesar showcased in terms of strength, power, and vulnerability. Perhaps the Orange Julius shows these characteristics better than any book could outside of an Edward Gibbon yawn fest. It is probably also important to mention Caesar's contribution to the role of dictator.

Julius was a man of the people, but more importantly he was a soldier. After a string of military victories against the Germans (previously known as the Gauls), Caesar fought with and eventually won against the Senate, which was led by Pompey. This culminated in the famous "Crossing of the Rubicon" which was eventually popularized in HBO's "Rome" series (OK, seriously HBO, give the author some swag.).

Fig. 2: Founder Of Orange Julius

Julius disbanded the Senate, or at least any power they had, and took complete control over the empire. He did his best to please the people with military victories, parades, gladiatorial combat, and ice cream Fridays. Eventually, his dictatorship angered those in the "castrated" Senate who wanted to steal from the people themselves. Corruption won out in the end when a group of Senators, led by Caesar's best bud, Marcus Brutus, back-stabbed him by literally stabbing him repeatedly in the Theater of Pompey, while also not inviting him to their sleepover later that day. No one can say for sure which of those led to his death. Julius would pass, but democracy would continue – for the time being, at least.

NAPOLEON: TOWERING ABOVE THE REST

First off, let's get this out of the way. Napoleon was not short for his time. He was a normal height, and deeply rankled by the British propaganda (well done, chaps, by the way). His propagandized stature didn't stop him from claiming authority over two thirds of Europe in his lifetime. Like his Roman predecessors, Napoleon relied on his military connections and prowess to become the de facto leader of France by the end of the 18th century.

Bonaparte used a coup d'état [see more on how to do this in Chapter 7] to shut down the government and become the "first consul" over the next decade. Unfortunately, Mr. Bonaparte made the first mistake that another dictator would later make and tried to invade Russia. He would eventually lose 100,000 troops from starvation, exposure, and better jobs that paid above minimum wage. This stretching of his army would be the beginning of his downfall as a leader and eventual exile. He also forgot to pay his Spotify family subscription and angered his Generals, the freeloaders that they were, who subsequently had to listen to Belgian advertisements.

MUSSOLINI: A FASCIST FACELIFT

Pedantic historians may disagree, but Benito Mussolini is often considered the founder of fascism. Hitler copied most things from Mussolini, including his governmental approach and his recipe for pesto. Fascism brought a sleek new feel to authoritarianism for the 20th century. It was like chrome on a Ford Pinto. That feel was total and complete indoctrination the people from birth.

Mussolini took power in 1925, following several years of his Fascist party gradually taking over the country. He immediately began to institute uniform propaganda. Within a year, all screened movies were fascist (including such greats as *Sun*, *Nerone*, and *Driving Mrs. Daisy*), 75 percent of media was Fascist, and most schooling had instituted compulsory classes promoting Fascism.

Unfortunately, Benito and his troops were better at fighting each other (and a few African countries such as Ethiopia) than anyone else in the world. They would steadily lose ground in WWII. He and his wife attempted escape in 1945 to Switzerland, but were betrayed, killed, and hung up for citizens to whack like a piñata. As the Fresh Prince of Bel Air would say, "[their life] got turned upside down."

PUTIN: THE MODERN AUTHORITARIAN

Talk about a guy who just won't quit, Vladimir Putin has been more-or-less the sole leader of Russia since 1999. A former KGB operative, and product of the Cold War, he would rise through the ranks: Colonel, Mayoral Advisor, Late Night Shift Manager at Arby's, and Deputy Head of Management. He would be appointed leader of Russia by Boris Yeltsin after the latter stepped down in late December of 1999.

While there have been dozens of dictators that have cropped up across the world, Putin remains one of – if not the – top of the proverbial crop. His vice-like grip on the extensive resources of Russia (many of which power half of Europe), his ruthless oppression stemming from his days at the KGB, and his ability to stifle any threats have kept him in power – and extreme wealth – for over two decades.

Putin is notorious for his use of creative assassination techniques to remove detractors, even in other countries (as this author may soon learn). He has successfully invaded two countries and won elections by over 90 percent, sometimes more than 100 percent in certain areas. Today, he is one of the supermodels of authoritarianism. Think of him as the Claudia Schiffer of autocracy.

⊕ ✠ ⚡ ꗛ ☭

Are You Ready to Rule – You Better Be

The short history lesson is over, and it is time to take your test. This will give you the information to determine if you are ready to start (or continue) your journey toward absolute power. Don't fret if you do not answer everything correctly, the key is not just strength, but determination. If you can make it through the ramblings of the next few pages, you are more than halfway there. Think of it as an authoritarian Myers Briggs. Let's give you some of the answers for the questions, too. After all, you should learn how to tip the scales in your favor at every opportunity.

C. T. Jackson

What do you consider your greatest achievement in life?

Everything you have ever done is your greatest achievement. Do not be bound by these questions. However, if you want to provide some specifics, here are a few good examples that you can use:

- Founded a social media start-up that contributed nothing to society
- Won an Olympic gold medal in speed bowling
- Survived a meteor attack
- Crushed your enemies, saw them driven from battle, and heard the lamentation of their women
- Watched all of *The Big Bang Theory* in a single binge-watch and are still not brain-dead.

What do you enjoy doing in your spare time?

Think of things that you wouldn't mind doing in front of the camera to keep up the propaganda for your citizens. Physical activities are a must in this instance. Ride horses, practice that bowling (you did win an Olympic medal, after all), swim, engage in alley fights, become a master checkers player, and hunt the homeless. All will be important in your campaign and beyond.

Do you have any enemies?

No, of course not, you love everyone, and everyone loves you. This is a lie, but you don't want to give away your enemy list this early in the game. There will be plenty of time to do this through racist dog whistles, ad hominem attacks, and Fox News guest appearances. They are all basically the same thing in the end.

Do you want some enemies?

You will have some enemies in due time. For now, you should lie on this question. What is the point of being an authoritarian if you cannot crush your enemies? Regardless if they know or do not know it yet, they are your enemies.

What is your favorite vacation destination?

You can choose the beach, the mountains, Pyongyang, Chernobyl, or Disney World. Or you can be a true authoritarian and choose all of them. You will be able to steal enough from the coffers of your country [see more in Chapter 7] to build your dream home in every vacation destination or radioactive dump.

What is the biggest challenge you have ever faced?

There are no challenges that you didn't overcome with ease. Everything is easy for someone as perfect as you. Remember that time you fell off your bike? No you do not, because you never fell off your bike.

If you could only change one thing about yourself, what would it be?

Nothing. You are perfect and everyone else should know how perfect you are. If you truly had to pick, it would be that you are too kind to everyone.

What is your best memory from your childhood?

It was probably something traumatic. Why else would you be here after all? Don't take it as a bad thing. You can use it as an excuse for any unsavory behavior throughout your rule. Or you can push it down deep inside of you and never, ever talk about it again.

DO YOU HAVE A MORAL COMPASS? DO YOU KNOW WHAT A MORAL COMPASS IS?

No and no. What are you, a boy scout? You have GPS, so no need for a compass. Morality can be bought anyway.

WHAT IS YOUR GREATEST FAILURE?

Trick question! You have never failed at anything in your life. Congratulations, you are perfect; now harness that perfection into a successful campaign [see Chapters 6 – 7] and rule [see Chapters 8 – 10].

WHO IS YOUR ROLE MODEL?

You can look at the Appendix for plenty of role models, but a few good options would be:

- Josef Stalin (famous smallpox survivor)
- Joe McCarthy (famous communist hater)
- Joe Jonas (famous Jonas brother)
- Joe Montana (famous state)
- Joe Biden (famous old guy)
- Joe Rogan (famous idiot)

DO YOU WANT TO HAVE YOUR OWN QUIZ?

Too bad, go write your own damn book [see Conclusion for more].

If you answered everything with a "Yes" or "No" then you may have intelligence issues. If not, and you followed the advice for each question, then you are a follower and will struggle to be anything more than that. If you skipped this chapter and are just reading this paragraph, then congratulations, you are ready to pursue a career in despotism!

JOINING A STORIED HERITAGE

As you begin your long journey toward the halls of absolute power, know that you are joining a storied tradition of oppression. For thousands of years, great men – and some women – have worked hard to rule over their lesser. That tradition continues today as many countries are controlled by despots and dictators. Democracy continues to slide across the globe, continuing to open up possibilities for you to close down freedoms and rights.

Fig. 3: Opportunities Abound For The Aspiring Tyrant

As you can see, the lighter colored countries are already taken by your peers. Yet, there are still plenty of countries that are considered "free," which means many opportunities for you to stake your claim and join the ranks of great tyrants.

CHAPTER 3

PRACTICE MAKES PERFECT

"Infinite striving to be the best is man's duty; it is its own reward."

— MAHATMA GANDHI, FAILED NUTRITIONIST

No one woke up one day and became a dictator. It takes practice to get to Carnegie Hall, and it takes even more to overthrow the government building, rename it "Dear Leader Hall," and proceed to ban music entirely. So, you are going to need to start logging those reps if you intend to oppress the masses properly – especially the musicians.

Every aspiring authoritarian needs a rigorous schedule and discipline. Despite the oft-repeated phrase that so-and-so dictator isn't mentally or physically fit to rule, many of the most successful ones were authoritarian in their diets and physical fitness regimens.

Eating Right – Far Right

You aren't going to lead the masses to overthrowing their democratic chains from the couch. You will need to institute a diet – at least until you take power – then it will no longer matter.

Eat This:

- *Vegetables* – Yes, even Hitler ate his greens. In fact, that is mostly what he ate, and he took over most of Europe. So, open up, here comes the Luftwaffe plane carrying broccoli for landing.
- *Staple Foods* – Rice, lentils, beans. Keep yourself in line with the masses, those who will eventually lift you up. You will connect with your loyal supporters (i.e., subjects) by eating their peasant gruel.
- *Fresh Fruits* – You cannot catch scurvy before you take over your country. This is also a good way to connect to the nationalistic pride of your countryfolk. Choose fruits that are farmed in your country or choose locally sourced produce from the barren wastelands near your borders. If you believe Idi Amin, fruits – specifically oranges – grant sexual prowess. He ate 40 a day, and you know he got down with the ladies.
- *Humans* – You will need some protein in your diet outside of beans and lentils. Nothing beats "long pig" to satisfy your protein needs while removing potential detractors and competitors from your conquest. Fresh tip! Keep heads in the fridge so they last longer and can be brought out for fear mongering. Freezer bags will help keep even the earliest of your political enemies fresh long into your reign.

Don't Eat This:

- *Sweets* – Don't bother with cakes, cookies, and candies. While apocryphal, the "let them eat cake" rule of thumb from Marie Antoinette still applies here. Sweets are a known representation of class difference, and you don't have the luxury (yet) to flaunt your sweet tooth. In addition, a good dictator wins on a smile, and that doesn't work with rotten teeth. Go ahead, think of the last successful authoritarian with bad teeth. As horrible as they are, they generally have great, disarming smiles.
- *Breads* – This isn't about being a dictator; you just eat too many carbs. Sandwiches, while delicious, are not akin to a show of power. The destruction of your stomach lining from eating Subway products isn't worth the limited connection it will give you to the plebs. Bread is best used to throw to the masses as you show your sham support for their nutritional needs.
- *Fast Food* – This is an easy trap to fall into given the ample use of authoritarian or monarchical verbiage by many popular chains. Burger King, Little Caesar's Pizza, White Castle, Dairy Queen, and Saddam Hussein's Chicken and Waffle Shack all sound mighty, but you'll just end up flabby. That is not to say that you can't gorge yourself post-election, but you won't reach the top in sweatpants. Several famous despots have taken their fast-food cravings to the stratosphere. Human Cheese Puff, Donald Trump, notoriously provided McDonald's (still wrapped) on White House dining ware for his guests. Meanwhile, Kim Jong Un of North Korea suffered from "cheese-infused gout." For now, skip the drive-thru until you can drive there. Preferably over your enemies.
- *Foreign Food* – You cannot possibly expect to foster

nationalism in your followers if you are caught eating the dirty, unpalatable garbage of other countries. It is important that you stick to the native foodstuffs, no matter how disgusting they may be. Image is everything, as we will discuss later in the book, and pictures of you munching on exotic foodstuffs will hurt your persona more than you can imagine.

Fig. 4: Kim Jong-Healthy

A Good Fascist is a Fit Fascist

The saying goes that "abs are made in the kitchen," and so it goes for absolute power. However, you will really need to exercise those muscles if you are going to thump the podiums properly during your fiery speeches. It takes tight tendons to connect with your military. It takes strong calves to ensure you can turn a stiff heel on the civilian population. You need those pumped pectorals to be able to take off your shirt while riding a horse. There are several key exercises and sports that you can do to meet these fitness goals. Don't worry, once you gain power you can have others fake it for you. Remember, image is everything.

Swimming

You don't need to achieve Michael Phelps's level of fitness. You can always make your own Olympics and win those anyway. The key here is that, at its most basic level, swimming is relatively easy. You can mostly just float from one end to the other while feigning the most basic strokes to keep up the perception for your followers. Moreover, it provides a solid excuse for the fact you have installed an Olympic size pool in your presidential mansion. Mao

Zedong managed this while millions starved across the country. That's what we call a "breast" stroke of genius.

HUNTING

Some would argue that this cannot be categorized as a sport. Their opinion will be well noted as they are running through the jungle on your private island for hunting detractors. For some reason, humans have a penchant for guns. You do not need to go into the psychology of this "small dick energy" aspect. Just embrace it and leverage it to further showcase your strength. You probably don't have to actually shoot an animal, but you must pretend that you did. Fire into the air and edit the video to show your "kill" afterwards for the people. The most important part of this sport is to take lots of pictures with you holding various guns in a shooting position. Hunting is basically a boutique photo shoot with a 40 percent camouflage ingredient. Show the people what you got, with both barrels.

WEIGHTLIFTING

Probably the least sexy of the possible exercise routines you can do as an aspiring authoritarian. However, it is a strong candidate for the way to build your physical perception for the populace and makes for great pictures and videos with which to promote your image. Don't fret! You don't actually have to lift massive amounts of weight, just pretend you are doing it. There are plenty of places to buy "fake" weights if you need to crank out a few convincing TikTok videos. While it is good to keep an actual regimen until you are well into your infinite tenure as leader, a commitment to the perception is more important. This is also a good avenue through which to sell your faux protein and workout supplements to generate cashflow for your campaigns and bribery schemes.

Wrestling

This will probably apply to aspiring dictators in areas around the Mediterranean; however, there is an avenue here for the North American authoritarian, too. For those of you too lazy for this level of commitment, you may skip this section. The strength portrayed in traditional wrestling is a boon for any aspiring dictator. For the Greeks, it brings them back to a time when they weren't a complete mess and were actually feared. For the Russian peoples, it continues a long tradition of showcasing one's strength by not wearing a shirt. Pecs win votes past the Caucasus mountains. So grease yourself up, find a partner, and get to pinning them down. Pretend they are the masses that you will eventually dominate. Perhaps kiss them gently before making them submit to your will. Now THAT'S a metaphor.

For the North American reader, the World Wresting Entertainment, Inc. (WWE) is a chance to practice not only your shirtlessness, but also your charisma. While no WWE wrestlers have managed to conquer parts of the known world, the Rock (Dwayne Johnson) has managed to conquer jungle-themed Hollywood movies. So get your spandex ironed, inject a bagful of steroids, and develop your character to either befriend or anger the crowds. Either way, it will be great practice for the larger crowds you must appease in the future. Do you smell what the leader is cooking?

$$\oplus \maltese \maltese \maltese \maltese$$

Professional Development – Gain Valuable Experience

Now that you have your diet and fitness routine established, it's time to work on your professional development. This is the most important part of your training. Don't worry, no certifications are necessary to run a country, except for the one at the end of this book (for the bargain price of $349.99). In the interim, there are several positions that require almost no modicum of intelligence or experience but allow incumbents to flaunt an inordinate and undeserved amount of power. These positions are a great way to wade into "dictator mode."

HOA Board Member

There is no career that embodies the authorization mindset more than a board member of your local Homeowners Association. They are absolute power incarnate. If you happen to be a middle-aged white woman, read on. You are in the best position for practice in creating and enforcing arbitrary rules against an unwilling populace. For instance, consider delivering an exorbitant fine to a neighbor for painting their door the wrong color. Now, that is just a step away from jailing a neighbor for painting their door the wrong color. Same crime, different punishment. If you reach this level, you are already punching above your weight. Now punch down.

School President

Hello, child and future oppressor. Congratulations on your win in the school polls. I do hope you based your campaign on unachievable promises, popularity, and overall disparaging of the competition. You now have some semblance of power, although do not get too cocky. There is still an oligarchical administration and your parents to deal with. The key here is to flex your power to the extent you can. Promise ice cream parties, cancel dances, funnel the school treasury funds into your own personal purchases, then announce there is not enough for activities. The school has let the children make decisions for each other in a brilliant attempt to avoid responsibility. You too can avoid responsibility, as you are a child, so keep pushing the limits of your power.

Little League Coach

Hi, Dad. Let's assume you are a dad for this role, although Little League does not discriminate. That is your job. You have a fantasy role commanding the respect and attention of 11 to 20 children. Sports provide an excuse for parents to abuse their children and the children of their peers. For reasons beyond comprehension, other parents blindly accept any verbal abuse that a coach gives to their children. You need to capitalize on this attitude. These minor league minors are incapable of fighting back physically or verbally. It is up to you to push your agenda by promising rewards such as orange slices and Capri Suns, only for winners. This is also a good opportunity to pit the kids against each other by targeting weaker performers, praising the winners, and ensuring a healthy balance of peer pressure between them while you remain infallible. Physical sports are one of the best ways to placate the masses. Experience in this area will help an aspiring dictator such as yourself to push the right buttons during the rough times to assuage an angry electorate. The Romans perfected this with their gladiatorial little league series. Maximus was an amazing pitcher, who managed to win the championship with a ragtag group of slaves. Or was that *Bad News Bears*? Either way, you get the idea.

TSA SECURITY OFFICER

I get it, you need money. You cannot take over the country without a few greenbacks. Outside of the pathetic paycheck, you have basically been granted unlimited power to control all the scum who want to travel via flight. Outside of people from the highest levels of oligarchy, who take their private planes or NetJets, you are the gatekeeper and controller of the other 99.9 percent. There is great practice to be gained in this role as you can enforce entirely arbitrary rules. These rules provide a level of fake safety while also allowing you to penetrate nearly all areas of privacy for the sake of the country's protection. This will prove useful in your reign as you utilize this same mentality to push out laws that remove most – if not all – layers of privacy in the name of untested protection. You are the off-brand Trojan condom of the world, embrace it.

CULT LEADER

Congratulations, you are in the Magna Cum Dictator level of power already. Take your mortarboard and use it as a weapon to punish your followers. However, don't think too small. Don't be a little cult leader in a big pond, be a big cult leader in a huge pond. You have established a good niche for power, but you are neglecting your full potential, especially given that you already have a group eating horse paste or drinking off-brand Kool-Aid for you. Why not shoot for the stars? Incidentally, this is another good opportunity to shill your favorite, personally named, brand of horse paste and/or Kool-Aid to your current and future followers. While Joe Rogan is more-or-less an anthropomorphic, diseased thumb, he does effectively utilize the role of social media cult leader to pawn his wares. You should do the same and hopefully pocket a fair amount of money (or whatever the hell Bitcoin is) to further your quest for absolute power. The one hitch is that you must scale your cult to meet electoral needs. You may consider latching onto a Scientologist, Kashi Ashram, or Beyonce ticket that will give you the platform to gather, enrage, and unite the masses to your cause.

THE TINPOT TRIFECTA

Whatever your job, internship, or conquered position, your experience will help you develop the skills that will translate to your authoritarian needs in the future.

The combination of a solid diet, a photogenic fitness regime, and a job that allows you to flex some semblance of power is key to pushing yourself toward becoming a tinpot dictator. You have the foundational aspects now, but those are minuscule compared to your public-facing view.

CHAPTER 4

STYLE OVER SUBSTANCE

"I firmly believe that with the right footwear, one can rule the world."

— BETTE MIDLER, SANDERSON SISTER

One of the most – if not the most – important thing for current or aspiring authoritarians is portraying an image of strength, superiority, and panache. The words that you use and the content you promote are more or less meaningless in the grand scheme of your rule. They are short-term and you will pivot, change, or do a complete verbal turnaround on many of the things you promise to the people. However, your image will last and will be remembered throughout your rule. Your style as a dictator is a way to show your people who you are without saying anything of substance about "who you are" and who you care about. (Hint: you only care about yourself).

Before we go over your wardrobe, let's take a moment to determine the key characteristics you want to adopt as absolute leader. Below is a helpful guide to choosing the baseline traits that all dictators must display, along with a list of outlandish quirks with which you can choose to accentuate your overall persona to the people. These characteristics will help you build your following, excuse any erratic or bizarre behavior, and ensure your legacy for generations to come.

IMPRESS TO OPPRESS

Let's go over the baseline characteristics that every authoritarian needs to adopt.

CORRUPT

Probably a no-brainer at this point. You won't get far without abusing your power for further gain and acquiring illicit benefits to expand your network, funds, and influence to gain momentum in your bid for power and to hold onto said power. Corruption can come in many forms, and you should apply all of them. It is imperative to constantly exchange favors with underground elements and supporters to bolster your short-term bid towards power. You may eventually have to repay some favors, but for now, you can offer semi-false promises. Depending on the level of power you garner in the early years of your rule, you may be able to remove the partners before any repayment is required.

Bribery is a necessary part of corruption; they go hand-in-cash-in-hand. Some countries, like the United States, have mostly legalized bribery through corporate lobbying and the creation of large groups (known as "Super PACs") that function as monetary slush funds. During your initial rise to power, you should avoid any direct contact with these organizations. Instead, ask a contact – who then asks another contact (always ensure two degrees of separation) to start one of these groups and funnel the money through them to support your campaign, but also to support your ability to bribe other officials, military leaders, and high-level community representatives. As the great philosophers Wu-Tang Clan once said, "Cash rules everything around me." And so it does.

Media Darling

Even as far back as the days of "yellow journalism" fathered by William Randolph Hearst (renowned sledding enthusiast), the media has been a trite, sensationalist method for keeping the general public "informed." Despite this, you must befriend the soul-sucking journalists, editors, and bloggers who are your image megaphones. In today's world, the successful dictators befriend the news outlets. They go on TV for interviews with respected newscasters and interviewers, bribe journalists to give "softball" perspectives in their magazines and online articles and spend a few minutes on the late-night shows to "connect" with the common folk. Don't worry, you won't have to keep pandering to them; once you achieve your ultimate goal, the majority of these avenues will be shut down, banned, or forced to change their programming to exclusively promote your agenda and persona.

It is likely you will have to choose to run under one of the current parties in your country. Luckily, the media has mostly divided itself into bullhorns for whichever party it deems most beneficial to its bottom line. For example, Fox News is a terrific opportunity to blather on about socialism and other inane topics to get your base voters fired up for your shallow promises. Many dictators in the past have utilized this relationship to be weekly guests on a given network's shows. This is brilliant for getting your face and faux messages out there on a consistent basis to keep the public aware and excited about you as their next leader. Utilize these media outlets to get into power, then once you win, strip them of any semblance of sovereignty and have them push your own messages.

Charismatic

This is an absolute must if you desire absolute power. If you don't have this trait, then forget about conquering your country – much less the world. Even the most taciturn, filthy, and down-right ugly dictators exhibited a considerable amount of charisma with which to charm their peers, excite their supporters, and bully the opposition. Do you seriously think that Mugabe, Hitler, Stalin, Mussolini would have been successful without their charisma? They couldn't even make it into the JC Penny catalog. Charisma overrides ugliness. So, my Joseph Merrick, Elephant Man-looking friends, you are not forsaken. If you can get the masses of the world to listen, respect, and idolize you, despite your poor physical features, then you will go far in your quest for dominance.

Charisma means energy. Energy is shown through powerful hand gestures (to be covered in future chapters), increasing the volume of your voice in speeches at appropriate times, kissing babies, pretending to care about individuals when the camera is on you, apparently making TikToks (this won't age well), and videotaping yourself doing one of the fitness regimes we discussed earlier. In addition, you will need to utilize this charisma when you are catering to the real people of power, the elites. You will need this for social gatherings in the South of France, yacht parties off the Gulf Coast, hunting expeditions on your private human hunting island, and benefit fundraisers in Midtown Manhattan. You need to project a level of confidence in your bid for power as well as after you gain control of the country. As we have noted, people are inherently moronic, but you must use your powers of persuasion to attract these idiots to your cause. Utilize charisma to ignite the plebs, and to cater to the elites. You will be able to ignore their needs more and more as you consolidate your power.

Beyond the baseline characteristics required to dominate a people and country, you have an opportunity to decorate your self-image with other traits that you can carry with you throughout your reign of terror. Think of it like hanging shiny bulbs on your Christmas tree of hate and power.

SAVIOR

A classic. Religion has always been the opiate of the masses and regardless of whether you embrace one or not, the "savior" character is still very much part of any play for power. The peoples of the world yearn for a time in the past – and they yearn for a deliverer of their wants and needs. Most of the time, their wants and needs are racist, jingoist, or narcissistic in nature. The key is to promise that you will deliver the majority a new way of life that excludes those people that they fear, hate, or distrust.

A savior persona is a great trait to have in highly religious countries, but it can also be co-opted to other purposes that are non-religious in nature. Wrap yourself in the flag of your choice, sing a poorly written country song, and touch on your roots working in the fields or factories (don't let the truth get in the way of a good story here). You have risen from the pains, ashes, and depths to save the people. Pretend to save them now, then forsake them later. A savior is only as good as his or her words, and your word is garbage beyond election day.

Fig. 5: A Totally Not Paranoid Poster

Paranoia

Are you still reading this? Why are you following me? Who sent you? These are just a few of many questions that you can start rolling around in your brain as you slip into a heightened state of fear and distrust. Don't fret too much yet, paranoia is a sign that you are gaining momentum in your quest. Or it is potentially a sign that you have already completed your takeover. This is called a "late stage" trait, and most successful authoritarians acquire a certain level of it sometime in their life. With that said, never trust anyone. Your goal is to have others trust you, and eventually to betray that trust for your own selfish ends. Dictatorship is a one-way, poorly paved street.

VANITY

Get out your mirror, open that walk-in closet, and press on those teeth whitening strips. It is time to show the people how well-tailored, manicured, and pressed you are to reflect your power. You must do all of this without giving away your shallow fragility, of course. Even the most ardent communist dictators practiced a bit of vanity. Stalin certainly had a well-trimmed mustache in all his photos, and those uniforms didn't launder and press themselves.

SADISM

No kink shaming here, it's understandable. After all, everyone has urges, some are just backed by the state apparatus to achieve climax. Imposing pain, suffering, and humiliation onto others is an admirable characteristic for dictators. This often goes hand-in-hand with sadomasochism, so be careful with aligning to this trait too quickly and too strongly. In your early years, utilize sadism sporadically as its effects on the general populace can turn many of your potential centrist supporters off your message. Sadism falls into the "late stage" category of traits, one that tends to increase as your power expands and as your boredom rises. When you do find yourself in a sadistic mood, be creative! Sadism doesn't have to be all gloom and pain – at least not for the giver. There are plenty of fun, imaginative ways to torture your subordinates and detractors. Some are best to display to the public to further terrify anyone seeking to prevent your consolidation of power or to overthrow your "benevolent" rule. Waterboarding, nail pulling, forcing someone to listen to "Baby Shark" over and over, and other psychological punishments are all good opportunities to quench your sadistic desires. These will be discussed later in the book. For now, dream and write down your fantasies to remember for later. When you finally become the great leader, the only obstacle is your imagination.

STRONGMAN

This is dedicated to our brave veterans who put themselves in harm's way to fight our enemies abroad and blah blah blah. It's insincere but if you are a true military veteran seeking dominance, this is the trait for you. It is a key trait if you intend to take power through a junta (more on that later). Utilize your experience and – hopefully – your influence in the military to augment this trait and thus your candidacy and eventual absolute rule. There are many great authoritarians from the past who exhibited this trait for you to follow – Napoleon, Mao Zedong, and Captain Crunch (He started as a Captain, but he strongarmed his way into controlling the fruit-flavored cereal sector). If you do have the sway of the military, you also get the chance to organize grand military parades through the main city square. Tanks, missile launchers, and soldiers in potential goose step are a wonderful way to ring in your new administration, celebrate arbitrary anniversaries, or just show your power to neighboring nations. The world – and the military parade – is your oyster.

NARCISSIST

You are amazing. You are the best at everything you do and if anyone thinks differently, they are completely wrong. They deserve to be punished for their gross mistake. You are admired by all who look upon you, interact with you, and listen to your words of wisdom. You are entitled to everything that has come to you and if you haven't received those materials or accolades, then it is the givers who are wrong. The problems and struggles of the people are not your concern. If they were as amazing as you, they wouldn't be struggling. Any problems are the faults or failings of others; remove them from your sight or at least publicly punish them for their incompetence. They should also anticipate your needs and understand your strengths – of which there are too many to count. You aren't an asshole, you are an innovator, a breaker of barriers and norms, you are the cream of the crop. In reality, you are an arrogant piece of shit, but stick to the script.

This trait will help you throw blame on your sycophants – who will take it willingly. It will also ensure you never have to apologize or take the blame for issues in your country, regardless of your current leadership position. It can be dangerous to fly too close to the narcissist sun too quickly, but this trait will come in handy as you throw followers to the wolves in order to protect your power and your fragile ego. Again, you are amazing.

PARANOIA

How the hell did you track me down? Who sent you? Didn't I write this trait already? I'm on to you.

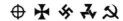

YOUR WARDROBE – WALK THE RUNWAY

With the boring characteristic aspects out of the way, it's time for the fun part – your wardrobe. Image, people, image. Learn it, love it, live it. It is time to check out the latest and hottest dictator-wear and get to showing off your style. Forget seasonal wear, you decide what is hot and what is not. If hot means traditional military wear for both spring and fall fashion, then it shall be for the next four decades. Let's start with some of the biggest names in authoritarian fashion that may soon line your golden closet.

MILITARY UNIFORM

Is that a military services parade in your pocket or are you just happy to see me? For military-inclined aspiring dictators, this is a solid choice for your everyday wear. In fact, it is likely you will don this on most public appearances. Any mere civilians reading this should not feel outcast; you can also make up your own uniform and wear it. However, be careful as you will not want to upset the delicate constitutions of the military. You will need their help regardless of your past military experience

Fig. 6: Big Hats Win Big Votes

The best part of the military uniform is of course the medals. You will want to adorn yourself with some legitimate, recognizable ones for the military populace. However, beyond that, you can make up your own and wear them without any civilian being the wiser.

PANTS SUITS

Communism gave the world many things: Gulags, The Red Scare, Proxy Wars, and Joseph McCarthy. However, perhaps one of the greatest gifts that it gave was the pants suit. Who would have thought matching blazer and trousers in the most rudimentary of styles could provide such a popular fashion trend across the communist authoritarians of the world? Many of the greats had closets full of pants suits – Victor Chavez in Venezuela, Mao Zedong of China, The Kim's of Korea, and of course the grandaddy of them all, Uncle Joe Stalin.

Fig. 7: A Typical Authoritarian Pants Suit

The popularity of the pants suits has waned in recent years, but like boot-cut jeans, tie-dye, world-wide plagues and any other fashion stalwart, there is always room for a comeback. You could be the catalyst for it. Make Throwback Thursdays a reality, and mandatory on all days for the people. Despite their rather plain design, there is room for adding your own flair to the suits. While the East Asian and Soviet Union dictators preferred a bare-bones model, the Latin American counterparts enjoyed a healthy number of pockets on both jacket and pants. Lest we forget the trademark hat that ties the outfit together, you can choose your brim and the amount of ruffle. Don't overdo it though. Remember, this is ostensibly a fashion choice that shows you do not need flashy suits and accoutrements. However, pants suits lead the eye down and away so you can avoid unnecessary attention while you gut the state for your own personal needs, comrade.

ITALIAN LEATHER

Connecting with the poor masses will get you far, but that is no reason to abstain from a healthy level of polish. This is particularly useful in the more stylish countries in need of the authoritarian boot-stamp of approval. This can also help you impress your fellow dictators at the annual BBQ. Did anyone see what Gaddafi was wearing last time? No one would be caught dead in it, and he sure wasn't.

Take a page from an oft-forgotten fashionista, Nicolas Ceausescu, former leader of Romania. He had his daily wardrobe sealed in plastic bags – now that is commitment. Ceausescu was famous for his tantrums, and he had a dazzling number of shoes in which to stomp on the ground in anger or kick the nearest peasant. You can get away with cheap knockoffs, but given the coffers at your disposal, it is best to go with the prime Italian brands. You will be the belle of the ball at U.N. functions (don't worry, they always invite everyone, though they can be fairly stuffy affairs). They will also be an eye-catching choice for fashion shows in Milan, celebrity shindigs, and at your eventual trial in the Hague. While everyone is staring at your shoes, you can pick their pockets and line your own – not too much lining though, that stuff is expensive.

Government Bureaucrat-Wear

Sometimes, a bore can bear fruit. And that type of dad joke goes great with a basic, achromatic attire. This dull style of wear is a perfect way to connect with the common folk as well as the face-less bureaucracy (i.e., middle-class) that will be essential to your rise to power. This is in no way disparaging the wonderful tailors that develop the clothing at Burlington Coat Factory; you are unrivaled in your craftsmanship. Bureaucrats are people, too. They make the world go round, albeit through unnecessary hoops, approvals, and form sheets. This lends you the opportunity, as a faceless bureaucrat, to rise above the gray and pointlessly legislate your way to power.

The commissars of Russia, the apparatchiks of post-Soviet satellite states, and the U.S. Office of Management and Budget (OMB) are prime examples of the power of the bureaucrat, and their clothing is a way to project that power even if it seems dull.

Fig. 8: Vladimir Putin Thinking About A Shirtless Cossack On The Steppes

Shirtless

Did you follow the fitness plan? How are those pecs looking? If they are "riding a horse on the tundra" worthy, then why spend your corruptly earned coffers on shirts? Your power comes with the pecs. The money saved can go toward anything you desire, as long as it doesn't trickle down to the people.

Accessorize Baby!

Don't walk out the door without checking your accessories in that full-length mirror. Make sure you bring or put on your accessories to fully complement your attire. There are plenty to choose from and they can give you that *je ne sais quoi*.

Sunglasses

These became a more fashionable item late in the 20th century. Perhaps it was a subtle way for authoritarians to bring awareness to the destruction of the ozone layer. Or maybe it was just to look cool while hiding their soulless eyes. Muammar Gaddafi was well known for his style and would often wear frameless, well-darkened shades throughout the day. Many African dictators – such as Robert Mugabe – opted for the gold-rimmed smaller frames. If you spent all your money on pants suits, maybe try and find some old "New Year's 2020" glasses instead.

WRISTWATCH

An aspiring authoritarian needs to keep well aware of the time as – for now – it is one of the few things you cannot control. You have plenty of options in the world today; perhaps go with Rolex, a favorite of communist authoritarians in South America like Fidel Castro. Or perhaps bring back the pocket watch, a favorite of Vladimir Lenin, and be the next hipster Hitler. No need to go overboard yet if you don't want to jam a bunch of diamonds into a Hublot watch. Go with the classic Casio, it even comes with a calculator! Now that is authoritarian efficiency.

FACE MASK

It is a brave new world out there following a global pandemic. Don't bother with whatever the government health agency recommends. Make your own style for the virus. If you are a fashionista, go with a lovely Louis Vuitton Ventilator 3000. If you are light on cash, just steal a Louis Vuitton Ventilator 3000. Whatever you decide, never wear the thing except around your wrist. You are strong and your people must always see your face; but at least you can feign a modicum of care for the safety of others.

SASH

Sashay Away as RuPaul would say. The sash isn't just for military leaders or diplomats from old 1920s movies. The best part about the sash is its versatility. You can mix and match colors and patterns and even emblazon your name or title across it. Easy to slip on as you are running out the palace door, it's a perfect, flamboyant addition to your wardrobe.

Spouse

Accessories aren't just inanimate objects, they can also be animate objects. Having a good spouse on your arm gives you likeability and something called "humanity." Plus, they often have strong fashion senses of their own. They can boost your image further this way. For instance, Imelda Marcos, wife of Philippine's leader Ferdinand Marcos in the 1980's, was known to have hundreds of pearls wrapped around her king-size bed for good luck. Another great example is Chantal Biya, wife of Cameroon's president Paul Biya, who had a social media group dedicated to her tall hair. Your best bet is to find a former or current fashion model, preferable an amoral one, who can help smooth out your image. Let's face it, if you are like most of the dictators in history, you probably look like a dog's breakfast yourself.

Your Carriage Awaits – Travel in Style

You've figured out your personality, your team, and your wardrobe. Now it is time to put all that together and travel to your campaigns and, eventually, between your political base and your luxury home(s). There is no need to choose between these travel styles, just pick and mix to meet your moods. Your needs will depend on your geography and your overall fear of flying and/or animals.

Helicopter

No, this isn't about helicopter parenting, you silly, upper middle-class white people. This is about the wonderful world of spinning blades to get insane rulers from their palace to the front lines and then safely back home. Let's start with the United States. Marine One is not a specific helicopter but the call sign of any choppers that carry the lord and savior of the Western world. The United States probably presents the fanciest way to walk to, enter, ride, and exit the Sikorsky flying machine. If you have the money to afford one – and let's be honest, you will after your win – definitely invest in a helicopter.

For decades, dictators across all continents have utilized helicopters for quick travel between their palace or compound to legislative meetings, or speeches to the people across the country, or most importantly, to their super yacht off the coast of Italy.

There are great opportunities for you to have speeches outside of the helicopter before boarding or talk to the media and not accepting any follow-up questions (assuming you haven't taken complete control of the media yet). Moreover, helicopter stairs provide one of the best opportunities (outside of airplane stairs) for photos to show to the people that you are off to negotiate, pontificate, or bloviate on their behalf. In reality, you are more than likely off to your private island, luxury villa in France or even your newly bought yacht with the Emir of Bahrain. Either way, it's going to look good to your citizens.

Bengal Tiger

Sure, people will laugh at you for riding a tiger to work. The first issue is that you do not work, you rule. The next issue is that there may be no tigers in your country. That is no problem, get two people to create a tiger suit and make it happen for you. Either way, you are riding an animal into your chamber for all to see. Many leaders have tried similar tactics. For instance, Stalin saddled a group of tied together communists to ride to Leningrad. Or Donald Trump, who rode Rudy Giuliani to his golden palace in Florida.

Public Bus

You are one of the people and are probably in the developing world. Are you seriously taking the bus, president of Peru? Fine. Stop reading from here on out. For the rest of you, don't follow the public bus leaders, there are plenty of other ways to fake activities that connect you with the poor without actually connecting with the poor.

Open-Top Car

Whether you are Adolf Hitler or John F. Kennedy, the open car is a great way to 1) hold a parade for your sake and 2) drive through that parade quickly while sending some love to the people.

Fig. 9: Open-Top Cars For Close-Minded Leaders

Although this didn't work out for one of these leaders, it still presents a great way to show yourself to the adoring crowds and travel in style. Hitler sat in the back of a Mercedes-Benz 770. It was well known that he never used a turn signal either, beginning the lofty tradition of Benz and BMW owners that has continued today. The great thing is that once you are in power, you will be free to run them off the road.

Kennedy chose an open-top 1961 Lincoln Continental four-door convertible. It was a slick ride and it looked good even with a president's brains on the back. Neural matter cleans up well with a bit of lemon juice and vinegar. When he wasn't being murdered, Kennedy enjoyed his ride across the country, and you can too if you decide to utilize this concept (very big in the corporate world today) to inspect your country.

Air Force Fun

Helicopters are nice, but why not have an entire jumbo jet at your disposal. There is an unlimited number of things you can do with your own 747 or – for the newer folks – a 787 Dreamliner. It has always been tough to bowl a perfect game on a commercial flight; now you don't need to worry about that. Beyond your bowling record, you have an opportunity to control your people from the sky. That is pretty cool. What is even cooler is forcing your people to work in the mines that help power all the circuits and gadgets inside the plane.

Fig. 10: Private Jumbo Jets Give The Zoftig Dictator More Space

An added bonus to having your own plane is that you can paint your name on it in giant letters, a flying homage to your growing narcissism. If you sign up for this option, you would be joining such prestigious jumbo jet owners as Prince Al Waleed of Saudi Arabia, Russian oligarch Roman Abramovich, and Iron Maiden.

CHAPTER 5

BUILDING YOUR PLATFORM

"Politics is when you say you are going to do one thing while intending to do another. Then you do neither what you said, nor what you intended."

— SADDAM HUSSEIN, IRAQ HIDE-AND-SEEK
CHAMPION OF 2003

Now that you have chosen your personality, implemented your diet and fitness regimen, and picked out your most dapper suit, it's time to establish your platform. The campaign trail officially begins today. Don't worry, this chapter isn't going to delve into the minutiae of sound plans for infrastructure, the economy, healthcare, or solving practical issues for your country. No, this is about maximizing your reach to your audience while catering to their base insecurities and hatreds. It is not about expressing complex thoughts on complicated issues. It's about black and white, us and them, and over-the-top promises that you will never follow through on. You've created your shallow, posturing, physical vision. Now, it's time to bring that same shallowness to your messaging.

Nationalism – An Authoritarian's Bread and Butter

Nationalism is basically libertarianism on steroids. Every nation should govern itself. The state government is the nation and vice versa. Many countries have sagged under the unruly nature of diversity. People tend to flock to those of similar characteristics – whether that be religion, ethnicity, language, politics, or sports teams. Nationalism is a way to bring all these different views under one umbrella, or rather one flag. However, you may want to avoid overtly nationalist overtures in your initial run up to the election. Instead, reframe it as patriotism. Patriotism is simply a combination of unnecessary flag waving and worship with a child-like view of your country as infallible. Patriotism is the gateway drug to nationalism. In fact, there is a simple formula you can use to fully showcase nationalism on your platform:

$$Patriotism \times (History - Atrocities)^2 + Foreign\ Enemy = Nationalism$$

You can also convert your platform ideals into your ruling principles after gaining power.

$$\oplus \maltese \text{ \$\ss\$ } \maltese \maltese$$

Once you have secured a polished set of nationalistic talking points, be sure to repeat them as much as possible. Even better, when your campaign opponents take the high road, immediately go low and accuse them of being unpatriotic. Let's go through a few examples of how you would answer some statements from your opponents.

"Globalism helps bring in new thoughts, ideas, and innovations to spur growth in the country."

Pass. Only your country and its people have the right to bring it. The country has all the right to those ideas and innovations, and they will grow from the faith of its people, not from malign foreign influences.

"Open borders and immigration help bring in a new workforce and diversity to the country."

Pass. You and your people didn't ask to be made into a minority in their own country. Immigrants also bring [Pick two: Disease, Drugs, Crime, Poverty, Anchor Babies, Hard Seltzers, Network Television Scripts].

"The country needs to participate in world bodies to help the lesser nations and contribute to global stability."

Pass. You don't need to contribute the country and people's hard-earned dollars, insights, and ideas to international organizations who offer no benefit other than crap like "world peace" and "helping people." Only your people matter.

⊕ ✠ ✞ ☩ ☭

Jingoism Unchained – Why Stop At Nationalism?

For some of you, it may be worth taking a step even further to inject a dose of jingoism into your campaign (although it is more prudent to utilize this after you have stolen victory). Jingoism is a more aggressive foreign policy model than nationalism, promoting the use of threats and military force to safeguard the interests of your country. Think of it as the proactive method of nationalism. Leadership coaches always say to be more proactive in life after all.

A popular song from late 19th century Britain epitomizes the early days of Jingoism:

We don't want to fight but by Jingo if we do

*We've got the ships, we've got the men, we've got the
        money too
We've fought the Bear (Russia) before, and while
        we're Britons true
The Russians shall not have Constantinople.*

Not the best rhyming scheme, but the point is well taken. Feel free to adapt this and replace Britain with your country and Russia with whichever arbitrary "enemy" you are targeting at any given moment. Perhaps improve on the rhyme – and get a TikTok dance to go with it? When you do claim power, why not adopt a dog with the name Jingo, or named with a racial slur for your enemies? There is no need for subtlety with the level of nationalism in your campaign.

$$\oplus \maltese \text{ ⚡ } \text{ } \text{ }$$

Gruel And Foie Gras – Catering To The People

There are two main groups of the populace you must patronize: the poor and the elite. With the former you must pander to their base desires and emotions in public, with the latter you must cater to their base wallets and thirst for power over the poor. This can be a delicate line as the two are clearly contradictory. The key to success is to never let your messages meet. In the age of social media and technology (to be discussed later), this can prove troublesome. Even if you do happen to get caught, say, hosting a fundraiser in a wine cellar, be prepared with public statements about the need for placating the rich in order to improve the lives of the majority (hint: this is a lie).

The Gross Poor

Well, there do happen to be more of them than the rich, as is traditional. They unfortunately have the right to vote – for now. So you are going to have to gain their respect, rile them up, and get them to the polls. These are actually fairly easy tasks, so long as you are unburdened by morality.

Gain Their Respect

You are a person of the people. Blue jeans, factory jobs, food stamps – you can pretend you had to deal with all of these to "connect" with the common man. You have toiled and suffered as a young tyke, working in the salt mines or whatever, it doesn't matter as long as it is relatable to them. In reality, your struggle was probably not being able to eat macaroni and cheese every night, or not getting that LEGO machine gun you nagged your parents to get you for the holidays.

Rile Them Up

ou are one with the people, and the enemies are all the people who have ever been better off than them. They sit comfortably in their villas or yachts outside the country, not paying taxes, and hob-nobbing with foreigners (all things you will end up doing in your reign). Don't dive too deeply into this part though, remember, those "enemies" are also your fundraising backers. Focus on attacking the outsider elites – the world governments, the enemy countries, and for an easy "alley-oop," the Jews (or any other minority denomination of your choice). They are the cause of all the problems for the poor. The lack of jobs, the rising costs of products, the lack of some unattainable utopia that rests in the heads of these people. There is no room for complex conversations on how the world economy works. It's so much easier to blame a single bloc of people.

Fig. 11: Riling Up Supporters Can Be Done By Even The Dumbest Of Dictators

GET THEM TO THE POLLS

More on this in the next chapter, but it is important to plant the seed as your campaign unfolds. The "outsiders," the enemies (whoever you decide they are), and the elitist cabals are going to rig the election, bus people in, or fake postal votes to win. You need to get the people mobilized and out there, most likely by doing the things you are accusing the other side of planning to do. Projection is the name of the game, and you will hear it often in this book.

$$\oplus \maltese \maltese \maltese \maltese$$

THE FANCY ELITE

They are the one percent, and they are the percentile that matters most. Call it an oligarchy or a plutocracy, the point is that you need it to build and sustain your campaign. According to science funded by Rich People Labs©, for every 1,000 poor and/or middle-class voters, you need one rich provider. It is not about the votes with this crowd. It is about the slush funds (e.g., Super PACs, Charities, Fundraisers) that allow you to push your message to the financially challenged voters.

Super PACs

This is mostly an American concept, but the idea may work in other countries, depending on their campaign finance laws. Without getting into detail, a Super PAC is a way to funnel money from the millionaires and billionaires into your campaign for use in advertisements to convince the poor you are one of them. Of course in reality, you use the bare minimum of these funds for campaign use and the rest goes into your personal slush fund.

Charities

Save the Children! Save the Lab Monkeys! Save the Whales! Save the Hybrid Monkey-Whale Children! Whatever you want to save, the only thing you are truly saving is extra cash for your campaign. It should all be funneled into your needs – and don't forget to take a cut off the top (those Italian suits don't pay for themselves). This is a nice balance between showing the people you care about issues (you don't) and a way for your elite backers to launder money through your charities and campaign.

Fundraisers

This may be the most fun part of your campaign. It isn't just about securing additional funds from the white-haired, half-dead aristocracy. It is about mingling with the rich heads of your country. These are the socialites, the heads of resource-grabbing firms, and the current legislators in the government. Fancy tablecloths, expensive champagne, silver utensils, it is all necessary for you to pamper the privileged.

They will pamper you back when you become the leader of the country.

An Example Fundraising Speech

Good evening ladies and gentlemen – but mostly gentlemen,

May I begin by acknowledging the traditional way we meet and to pay my respects to our forefathers, by eating overpriced shrimp and creating slush funds for politics.

I want you to think about the power that our country wields – what comes to mind?

We are an egg ready to spread its wings and devour smaller eggs.

We are ready to show the world that we are a beacon of strength, stability, sandwiches, sedition, spoils, and strongmen.

Our task is true and our reasons compelling. We must amplify our beacon. We are the caretakers of the rich and the corrupt – namely we care for each other.

We know what our task is and what needs to be done. But we need to make sure our people know why change is needed.

Our view is about empowerment, respect, and sameness. Just kidding, but don't let the plebs know that.

Therefore, I ask of you, help me to help the country. Help me show the people what we all see and strive for in the future. We are the wealth creators of this country. Let's help make it the way we want and not share it with anyone else.

It is why I recognize [name a few big donors here] in helping me secure the nomination and win. I will ensure your message is heard by me and is carried out.

Over The Top – Unachievable Promises And The Suckers That Believe Them

Promises are important to everyone, whether it be your spouse, a colleague on a project, or the person for whose sake you are getting tested for STDs. When it comes to leading a country, promises are the lifeblood of your campaign. Whatever is causing struggles or pain in your country, you must promise to fix it as leader. The best way to do this is to go above and beyond in your campaign promises. Even when people later complain that you haven't kept those promises, it won't matter. Especially when they are complaining to the other inhabitants of a political prison.

Now, you don't want to make promises so crazy that even the thickest of potential voters won't believe it. The critical task is to balance the challenges of the populace with a solution that seems reasonable, but in reality, is vague and fatuous. "I will implement this in my first year" is a great line to use. Hell, even American democratic presidents use that without any faith in the outcome.

Utilize your new platform to push out these unachievable promises. The more you promise, the more people will vote for you. Don't worry at this juncture how you will handle the disappointment the people will experience. There are simple methods to mitigate the anger from both the poor and the elite without you losing your reign. For now, you are focused on the present – and the present is a series of lies that helps you achieve your ultimate goal.

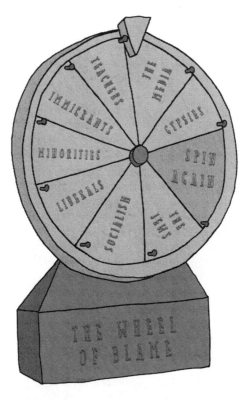

Fig. 12: Take A Quick Spin To Determine Who You Will Blame In Your Upcoming Campaign Speech

The Blame Game – Spin The Wheel Of Fault!

It is time to spin your way to blaming others for the issues your country is facing in today's world. This is imperative for pushing your agenda through the blaming of others while avoiding too many questions about your shallow agenda and lack of solutions to the real problems facing the country.

Teachers

Educators are a consistent, easily targeted enemy for the aspiring dictator. After all, they teach children about democracy, critical thinking, and encourage them to have a voice and to vote, those sick bastards. These lessons are all counter to your rule. Luckily, there are many well-tested methods for blaming the educators and the overall educational system. Countries like Turkey, Belarus, and the United States have mounted significant campaigns against their teachers in recent years to great effect. A key part of this blaming tactic is to target the parents so they take your side in viewing teachers as people who are trying to brainwash their children. This works extremely well with parents who have a limited level of education and a healthy distrust of the system.

IMMIGRANTS

They come over to our country looking for a better life for themselves and their families while taking the jobs that our lazy self-indulged people wouldn't do regardless of how they were paid. How dare they do that! It's time we sent them back and then complained when our fruit is left to rot on our trees and our lawns aren't mowed. All – or most – of the country's problems can usually be blamed on them. Or mix and match them with other groups to blame, it's your campaign after all.

THE MEDIA

Jewish World Order – The Bilderberg Group, The Cabal, George Soros, New World Order, Jimmy the Jew and His Antichrist Crew – this conspiracy goes by many names. Feel free to choose one or more when using them for your Blame Game. What good authoritarian doesn't have their "Blame the Jews" card in their wallet? [See the end of this book to save 25 percent on your "Blame the Jews" starter kit.] Leverage the conspiracy theories; the fringes of both sides (or multiple sides if you live outside the States) tend to fall for them. This is usually a good way to bring in supporters from all sides. Say what you want about the conspiracy crackpots, they do show up to vote and they are experts when it comes to social media memes – the lifeblood of today's modern authoritarian.

The Jewish World Order

The Bilderberg Group, The Cabal, George Soros, the New World Order, Jimmy the Jew and His Antichrist Crew – this conspiracy goes by many names. Feel free to choose one or more when using them for your Blame Game. What good authoritarian doesn't have their "Blame the Jews" card in their wallet? [See the end of this book to save 15% on your "Blame the Jews" starter kit]. Leverage the conspiracy theories; the fringes of both sides (or multiple sides if you live outside the States) tend to fall for them. This is usually a good way to bring in supporters from all sides. Say what you want about the conspiracy crackpots, they do show up to vote and they are experts when it comes to social media memes – the lifeblood of today's modern authoritarian.

Socialism

What is socialism you ask? Don't worry about it. It can be whatever your heart desires and your mind can imagine. It can be food stamps, healthcare for the less fortunate, equal pay, equitable taxes, or Bernie Sanders in a flaming red jump suit. It doesn't matter. Here is a simple way to push this message.

"[BLANK] is Socialism. [BLANK] infringes on Freedom or Liberty. [BLANK] will destroy our way of life."

That is it. Replace [BLANK] with whatever you want and you have sullied that person, place, or thing for the foreseeable future. Be sure to sprinkle the term throughout your campaign and blindly throw it against opponents and their messages, no matter how reasonable they may sound. This strategy is most effective in the United States, but it never hurts to try in other countries.

Minorities

This is a slightly different take than just blaming immigrants. This may overlap with several of the other categories, but that is

OK. It's all OK when it comes to the Blame Game. Some good messages to attach to this group are often around "stealing welfare," "not paying their fair share," "higher levels of crime," and just your general dog whistle racist undertones. You don't have to believe any of it, as long as your mindless supporters do, then it will boost your bid into office. After all, aren't dictators the real minority here? There are just so few of them.

Gypsies

For some reason, everyone hates gypsies. Doesn't matter if they even exist in your country, people despise them. Lean into it, blame those "Romani" with their beautiful culture and treasured love of travel for all the problems of your country, even if the gypsies live thousands of miles away.

Liberals

This may not apply to all of you, perhaps you are utilizing a liberal ticket in South America as an avenue toward power. If so, just replace "Liberals" with "American Capitalists." That often works wonders down there. For the rest of you, always blame the progressives, the ones who actually care about their constituents. They are the most dangerous because they may get elected and cause real change. Oh who are we kidding, they can't get past primaries. Either way, blame them as an entire, generic blob of evil. Take on the traditionalist view of your country and claim the liberals are aiming to take that away by bringing in immigrants, empowering minorities, and controlling the media. Just like that, you've tied in three other groups as well. Don't get greedy though.

Discrediting Your Opponents – Personal Is Public

You are infallible, remember that. They are full of faults, mischaracterizations, and hypocrisies. Keep that mantra in mind. The field of candidates is narrowing, you need to attack them. Forget showing your position at this point, attack their positions. It works better with the people. Negative advertising against opponents has been proven to be more effective at garnering votes than positive advertising for yourself. Utilize the points of nationalism, jingoism, targeting foreigners and internal enemies to push out your message. Most importantly, you need to utilize ad-hominem attacks and target your opponent's personal life to win support.

Reaching Your Audience – Tweet To The Top

You have your platform, your allies, and your enemies to blame. Now you need to get these messages out to your people. Luckily, Silicon Valley has provided a number of ways to easily reach even the poorest of people through the wonderful hellhole of the internet. A successful dictator in today's world is at least somewhat tech-savvy or has an entourage who can provide that level of savviness. For the retirees reading this, ask your grandson, granddaughter, or your underpaid Filipino nurse. There are several avenues on which to push your message to the people and help them augment your message, stifle those messages of your opponents, and ostracize minorities who disagree with your rule. Isn't social media fun?

Twitter

This will be your main mouthpiece. Understand it, love it, embrace it. All traditional news media will base their stories on your tweets because that is where we are as a species today. Your messages need to balance a degree of subtlety with blaming the undesirables and riling up your base. Be careful here, too much can get you banned, and only total idiots do that, like former U.S. presidents. What you want to do is keep your message relatively clean and let a growing group of racist aunts, eastern European bot farms, and nationalist trolls add their own context to it through other social media forms.

FACEBOOK

It is hard to believe that this application developed by the lizard people's king was originally used for something as stupid as connecting with friends in college. Thankfully, the lizard needed more and thus the world of Facebook opened up for dictators to exploit the platform. And you will, too. Take the initial message(s) from your tweets, place them over an irrelevant image and unleash the racists, rednecks, Facebook boomers, trolls, and Russian bots to bolster your cause.

INSTAGRAM

In the early days, you will want to control this medium yourself. Post generic quotes about leadership, endurance, and over-coming adversity. Put these quotes over non-threatening back-grounds and that should win you over plenty of fluffy new supporters.

Fig. 13: Deep Thoughts From Former Ugandan Dictator, Idi Amin

As your campaign gains momentum, you will need to pass these duties off to a subordinate. While an intern will do in a pinch, you need to ensure your message gets maximum views. You will have to enlist the service of an "Instagram Influencer."

The categories in the "Blame Game" are downtrodden or distasteful groups you must victimize for all problems. However, the only category who are more genuinely vile, more wretched, and more useless than them are the "Instagram Influencers." They are the Mos Eisley of people. Yet, they are useful in your bid for power on this platform. Provide them with some free campaign swag and promise not to jail them after your victory, which should be enough to secure their services. After the election, the purge can begin.

TikTok

Unfortunately, the younger generations have begun to reach voting age. Thankfully, it is far easier to bet on their apathy and lack of attention to ensure they fail to show up at the voting booth [more on that in Chapter 6]. However, it a waste not to take advantage of their preferred medium. Times change, but most of the unwashed masses still want a "cool" leader.

No need to come up with anything original on your own, this isn't about creativity. It's about emulation and timing. Have one of your media interns scour these social media dregs to find the latest hit and get to work emulating the dance. You have no time to lose, the trends on this format can be measured in nanoseconds. Debase yourself. It won't be the first time nor the last time. Do whatever is needed, spout out your message and watch it spread like wildfire. You may choose to nationalize the service and use it to pull data on your subjects later in your reign, so it is good to have a baseline familiarity.

YouTube

The original video upload service is at your disposal. There are two ways you can capitalize on this platform.

1. Actual Videos – Like and Subscribe! Apparently,

these are the only two words that matter. You can upload campaign advertisements, personal videos (e.g., staged ones that show how cool you are or how much you are a family person), or simply videos that engage with the current zeitgeist. The YouTube group ranges across age groups, unlike TikTok and Instagram, so it is definitely necessary.

2. YouTube Ads – This platform requires freemium users to listen to at least one 10-14 second advertisement without skipping. This presents an opportunity to blast your message on these ads over and over. Do not worry if people get sick of seeing your face before each video. They may hate you in the moment of preventing their instant gratification from the latest Marvel trailer, but they won't forget you. That is all that matters when getting these idiots to vote - who was the most recent person they have seen.

Twitch

This is a must for the gaming enthusiast and authoritarian. For the rest of you, this is probably a necessary "once off" to get a certain group of young people on your side. Yes, the young people are mostly useless, but garnering their attention by streaming your game will get them to stand up from their $300 gaming chairs and vote for you. The widely abused Alexandria Ocasio Cortez (AOC) has utilized this platform to her advantage and she was already elected. If a progressive liberal can do it, so can you.

Remember, it is not about controlling the media. It's about maneuvering it to your needs during the campaign and beyond. These methods allow you to establish control more easily and help push the public to your side. Or better yet, use these methods to push them against your opponents. The use of these methods will be paramount to securing your victory as election day looms just over the horizon. Your time is now.

CHAPTER 6

IT'S ELECTION DAY!

"It's not the people who vote that count, it's the people that count the votes."

— JOSEPH STALIN, AKA THE HUMAN MUSTACHE

The day is finally here! [Note: If you decide to gain power through a coup, feel free to skip to the next chapter. Although you may want to utilize these skills in any future faux elections that you hold.]

The polls are about to open, and it is time to see if your hard work has paid off. If in the early hours it doesn't seem to be paying off, then it's time to take some action to ensure it does. In fact, the power of election day starts long before the ballots are cast. You may have already discovered this in the previous chapters, but it is a good time to drive these points home now.

DISENFRANCHISEMENT – NOT JUST A RIVER IN EGYPT

What better way to thwart voters than ensuring they cannot vote for anyone in the elections? This is a tough act given you currently have no power. However, if you played your early cards right, you should have influence with local officials. In the months leading up to the election, there is ample opportunity for you to lobby for arbitrary laws that place obstacles in front of the less fortunate and the less desirable. In fact, it's important to review these potential laws now.

UNNECESSARY REQUIREMENTS FOR IDENTIFICATION

A simple picture identification card isn't nearly enough for this election. Voters need to also have a valid bill with their home address, passport, and a fully loaded Dave & Buster's Power Card. Not enough game credits? Then you ain't voting.

SORRY STUDENTS

College students are an aspiring dictator's worst enemy. They tend to know things and to have some semblance of critical thinking, especially if they went to a non-state school. Make unreasonable requirements for them; are they from out of state/province? They have to make their way back to their home to vote. Do they only have a student identification? Sorry, that can get them discounts at bookstores, but it disqualifies them here.

PROBLEMS WITH PROBATION

Expand the ex-felon voter restriction laws to include anyone who has been convicted of a misdemeanor, speeding ticket, or had a parking violation. Don't worry, you can ensure your loyalists with any past transgressions are exempt.

Public Transportation, Friend and Foe

This is a two-for-one tactic. First, you ensure your poorer supporters are bussed into the districts by paying for fleets of school or private buses to get them to the polling place. Second, you utilize these supporters to block the alternative public transportation options available to your opponents. Perhaps you have even developed connections to help "delay" these modes of transportation. You might want to disable all those goddamn city scooters too. Not just for election day, but forever.

Fig. 14: A Typical American Voter ID Card

Disabled? Disqualified

Strange how all the polling places have stairs. Crazy how all the sidewalks are blocked off for "construction". Odd how episodes of *Young Sheldon* are suddenly on televisions everywhere.

Voter Intimidation – Harassment Ain't Just For The Police

Every breath you take, every move you make. Be sure that you are watching them. Be sure that they know you are watching them. Be sure that others know that you are watching those people that need watching. Be sure... well, you get the idea. To quote the well-known voter intimidator, Sting [Note: Our lawyers informed us that actually quoting Sting in this context could result in legal action, so we need to state emphatically that this is a joke], "I'll be watching you." This should be an important message in your campaign in the most – yet least – subtle way possible. Just like the song.

Fear is a significant motivator for humans. For instance, this author is fearful of the wrath of Sting and has thus stopped writing about him. The "Fight or Flight" response has defined the way humans act and react to specific events and stimulants.

Your key as an aspiring dictator is to activate their "Flight" response. This is far easier to manage than the "Fight" response. There are several ways to use this to prevent voters from even showing up to the polls. If you cannot keep them at home, then there are ways to turn them away if they do try to get in the door of that elementary school.

A note here: These next sections, while addressing the aspiring dictator, are mainly meant for the subordinates, sycophants, and college interns who will carry out these tasks for you. Therefore the "you" is collective, but not in that stupid communist collective sense. Unless you are aiming for that, then go for it as long as that is your vibe.

DISRUPT THE DAY

Sow confusion. This works great for the older generation. Any public record can give you voter registration details; use it to send pamphlets with the wrong dates for voting. Uncle Al might want the moderate candidate, but he is coming to cast his vote during second grade math class a week too late.

SCARE THOSE WHO CARE

Lions, Tigers, Terrorists, Minorities, and Bears, Oh My! Cast a terrifying view of the poll environments for potential voters. Many might not truly believe there are Islamic lions waiting to hurt them at the polls, but it will be enough to keep them in their homes and not risk it. This is often an easier course of action.

MUDDLE THE DIRECTIONS

A risk, but a fun one if it pays off. The voters know the day, so rather than lie about that, change the venue. Find the other party's voters and send them directions to a different "polling place." It can be a closed church, a school that doesn't exist, a Total Landscaping company parking lot, or maybe the local Dave & Busters. They will have their Dave & Buster's voting card, at least.

Fig. 15: A Sign That Leads To Nowhere

DISTURB AND DISORIENT

If you have the ability, why not just shut down all possible avenues for voting. This goes beyond just the transportation disenfranchisement. Fake a fire. Better yet, fake a meteor hitting the earth, or hold a giant block party across neighborhoods. It doesn't matter how you do it as long as you block any routes to the polling place. Hell, that probably isn't even illegal in most places, not that it matters to you in the end.

Early Thanksgiving – Stuffing A Ballot Box

It is often amazing that something as important as the decision on the head of the future government is reliant on a cardboard box and pieces of flimsy paper. But here we are. There cannot possibly be a way to exploit this foolproof method.

So, here are a few ways to exploit this foolproof method. Get your piece of paper out and take notes.

Lift and Shift

It is that easy. Well, not that easy. You will need to have one or two lookouts while you pull up the top and either add new, fake votes into the box or pull out the legitimate votes already cast inside. This is often easier toward the end of election day.

Double Dip

Is it twins? Triplets? Doesn't matter as long as they all vote 20-30 times in multiple districts, they can be whatever you want. It is certainly easier to have connections with the poll workers to allow your "triplets" in to vote. If you cannot manage that, then best to map out the election stations and have a few fake IDs at the ready. Most poll workers are older and volunteers so it will be easier to get past them. Except Phyllis, she is terror incarnate.

The Early Bird Gets the Victory

If you are truly a go-getter, then get the voting boxes before they get to their elementary schools and other polling places. Fill them with your absolutely, non-contested, totally legitimate votes before they are set out for the day. It really isn't a major challenge to find the mini vans that deliver the boxes to the polling places. The author would suggest asking Phyllis, but that jerk won't even text back. She will get what is coming to her soon enough.

After School Special

OK, so you woke up late. You still have time to stuff those boxes (hold the giggles). Get your goons to the central polling collection area. There is usually one for each district. If not, you will have to spread out and conquer.

Now you might be asking, aren't these methods obsolete because of technology? Have you seen how well that has worked in the last few years? The future is now and the now is the past. And the past is the future. And my stroke is happening right now.

Paper voting is like that obstinate grandpa who is nearing 103 years old and continues to smoke cigarettes and throw back whiskey sours. It just won't die. So rather than try to kill it or get it to do yoga and drink more water, you exploit it for your own gain in its twilight years. Hell, it will be dead soon anyway.

$$\oplus \; \maltese \; \mathcal{S} \; \maltese \; \mathcal{R}$$

Get Out Of The Way – Obstructing The Opposition

Adding your votes is only half the game – and it is a game. The other half is ensuring the votes of your opponents are minimized or better yet, eliminated. A similar effort is needed from your subordinates.

Burn, Baby, Burn

There is some collateral damage here, but does that really matter? Rhetorical question. It doesn't. Due to legal concerns, this book cannot recommend burning down an elementary school or the papers inside. However, if an errant match ended up being accidentally lit and that lit match ended up on a box of paper that happened to have names written down who happened to be running for an election that happened to be apropos to the needs of the country and it happened to be that the name of one person was on a majority of those pieces of paper and that person was your opponent. Well, that would be such a tragedy.

CRISS CROSS, CROSS OUT

Well, let's take a look at these pieces of paper. It seems that there is one name that is attracted to the black Sharpie – or even better the X-acto knife. Wow, can you believe that all these voters marked a black, empty space for their candidate? That is even stupider than the ones that marked their vote for the Libertarian candidate. It is a shame that their voter cards have to be discounted.

HIDE AND NEVER GO SEEK

It can be painstaking to remove names individually. Isn't there an easier way? Of course, there is! If you had a childhood – and you might not have, given the readership of this book – you may have played Hide and Seek. It's easy, but here are a few examples just in case you struggle with where to put them:

- *A Sewer.* All the votes float down here, you will too. You will too.
- *Wherever They Buried Jimmy Hoffa.* Any ideas where that might be?
- *A Cemetery.* There are plenty of holes for lots of votes to fit in there. You just need to dig up a few bodies. This may feel strange as, for most dictators, the aim is to bury the bodies.
- *In Your Body.* You can eat those votes, or well, there are other avenues.
- *A Wardrobe.* You can have a lion and a witch guard it for you, too. Just watch out for nosy British brats.
- *An Indiana Jones-Style Government Owned Warehouse.* There are top men working on the votes. Top. Men.
- *Literally Anywhere.* You can put these boxes of votes

in almost any area that is open, the voting police aren't going to find them. It's doubtful they will even look for them for very long before giving up.

- *Hide the Entire Polling Place.* Now you are thinking outside the voter box. Why bother with hiding a whole bunch of votes when you can simply shutter the polling place or move it without telling anyone? The Georgia GOP did such a great job of this that even David Copperfield would be impressed.

DISTRACT POLL WATCHERS – SHINY BAUBLES OF DEMOCRACY

You still need to divert the attention of the many poll watchers. They are a different breed than the volunteer poll workers who are composed mainly of retirees looking for some semblance of attention. No, these are the watchers. They are trained by the strictest organizations of international elections. They come from the United Nations, the International Election Observation group, the International Election Fun Time Jamboree Team... OK, that last one was only just created, but it's still dangerous. These are the people who care enough to look. They are the biggest challenge to your actions – which are totally legitimate – during election day.

NO BADGE, NO PROBLEM

There he is, wearing a laminated badge, attached to a finely manu-factured nylon lanyard, hanging delicately around his neck. Take it. Take it and run as fast as you can. It is honestly that easy. International election bodies care about their badges more than anything. It is their identity. It is how they manage legitimacy. Isn't it funny how so small an object has so much power? Like some sort of ring of power even. Boromir didn't think kindly of election observers either.

Look Over There

Yes, a simple game you play with your three-year-old or with the gas station you are shoplifting from works well with the election observer or poll watcher. Distract them for long enough to steal a ballot box or even a pile of already filled out votes. Most watchers and/or observers lack object permanence and thus will forget what happened the minute you leave the gymnasium or hall of the elementary school.

How is Your Family Doing

Intimidation has so many creative outlets. A good one is to threaten a poll watcher or observer with the simple phrase of "How is your [spouse, brother, sister, daughter, son, grandparent, parent] doing?" You may have your people watching these relatives or you may not. It does not matter as long as they think you are in contact with them. There is a simple harmony in that inquiry that sends a chill down the spine of any volunteer. Feel the power as you make them feel the fear. Nothing like scaring a volunteer.

Thank You For Your Service

Sometimes you catch more flies with honey. Many of you think that "Your Service" is a military term. It is. But you can use it for anyone because you are being disingenuous anyway. Thank the postman for their service. Thank the volunteer retiree for their service. Thank the voters – but only your voters – for their strength in reaching the polls. Thank your subordinates, but not too fulsomely in case they get funny ideas.

Gaslight, Object, Project – The First Returns

The clock has hit the final mark. The votes are "cast." The counting begins. No need to sit back and wait for your totally legitimate win. It is always good to have a backup. It is time to start claiming that the election was fraudulent.

Not My Vote

There is no way that many votes came in during this election period. There is no way that that many votes were cast for your opponent(s). There is no way that those votes came in that quickly (Object).

Are you getting the idea yet? Those are all things you and your lackeys did. (Project). Well, you didn't actually do them. Someone else did. You cannot be blamed for those inaccuracies. It was clearly your opponent that miscalculated aspects of the election. (Gaslight).

Just Desserts

The narcissists' prayer is apt for this part of election day.

THAT DIDN'T HAPPEN
AND IF IT DID,
IT WASN'T THAT BAD
AND IF IT WAS,
THAT'S NOT A BIG DEAL
AND IF IT IS,
THAT'S NOT MY FAULT
AND IF IT WAS, I DIDN'T MEAN IT
AND IF I DID, YOU DESERVED IT
AMEN

It is a foolproof prayer and strategy for yourself on election day. Try to keep to the first line, but you always have a few backups if all else fails. Use this prayer wisely; it will come in handy further into your reign. The people deserve what they get and if they aren't willing to fight for it, then it is their fault and your gain.

Did You See What They Did?

Doesn't matter if it's true or false. Most likely it is false, but by being proactive in blaming the other candidate (or candidates) you have the public on your side, or at least against the other candidates. Against the other candidates is also on your side. This is the time to take the tactics explained earlier in this chapter and turn them around. Blame the other side(s) for trying to exploit, sabotage, or invalidate the election. Project everything that you and your cronies have worked towards against your opponents. This is also a nice way of seeing your work publicly recognized, albeit through the blaming of another candidate. Rigging an election is a humble act, one that garners no fanfare. It is basically Buddhism. [The author's lawyer has informed him to denote that this in jest, lest he is sued by the reincarnated form of the 12th Llama, who is the most litigious Llama].

Feign Legitimacy, Become Legitimacy

It is time to declare you are the ultimate winner of the election. Sure, it is only halfway through the day, but there is no time like the present.

This action is of huge importance as it forces your opponents to go on the defensive and say things that make them sound like losers, such as "Let's wait for all the votes to be counted before we make decisions." This, of course, plays right into your hands if you handled that pesky vote situation earlier in the day. It will come off as disingenuous if your opponents suddenly claim fraud in the votes. That is when you retort with a defense of the democratic process, counting of votes, and overall legitimacy of the election. You have now begun to establish talking points and your stature as a leader who will honor the democratic system (wink wink).

YOUR WIN PERCENTAGE – TOO MUCH IS NEVER ENOUGH

The 90 percent mark of winning votes has often been labeled by foreign policy experts as the demarcation between fully authoritarian governments who want to feign legitimate elections without truly caring about it. If you are above 90 percent – you couldn't give a shit about the international – or local – perspective on legitimacy. Below 90 percent, you are at least attempting to feign legitimacy in the elections.

Many of the authoritarian leaders in the former Soviet Bloc bat for the fences when it comes to their winning votes in elections. For instance:

Gurbanguly Burdimuhamedov, Leader of Turkmenistan – won with 97 percent of the total vote in 2012. He wasn't satisfied with that measly number and in 2021, he won the election with 100 percent of the vote. Now that is a go-getter, A+ student right there.

Fig. 16: Gurbanguly, A+ Student of Vote Win Percentage

Mikheil Saakashvili, Former Leader of Georgia – won with 96 percent of the vote in 2004 after his successor was ousted in a coup. However, after two successful terms of economic strength coupled with political and social repression, the coward admitted defeat in a follow-up election. Don't be a loser like Mikheil.

Jacques Chirac, Former Leader of France – won 82 percent of the vote in the 2002 election. This is one of the few landslide victories that was actually legitimate. It is so bizarre, but worth mentioning in case you end up with an opponent as truly awful as a "Le Pen" or a "Jill Stein." These are rare, but important to recognize if you and your team can see it coming. No reason to waste your time, labor, and money paying to rig the election if you can win it on the absolute incompetence of the other candidates.

Ronald Reagan, Former Leader of the United States and Current Zombie-fied Fetish Doll of the GOP – won with 49 out of the 50 electoral states in the 1984 election against the wet-dog-smelling rag, Walter Mondale. Again, no foul play needed, just a completely inept opponent. Reagan would go on to solve economics and save the downtrodden Wall Street executive.

Vladimir Putin, Current Leader For Life of Russia – While Mr. Big Chest has managed to win elections without the obvious 90+ percentile of the vote, he has achieved some great regional wins in previous elections. In 2012, during his presidential campaign, Vlad managed to win 107 percent of the votes in Chechnya. He won with a combined total of 1,482 votes to 1 for his opposition. This is even more amazing given the fact that the area only had 1,389 registered voters. Clearly Putin is some sort of shirtless sorcerer, and it would be good to learn his magic for your future "elections."

⊕ ✚ ⚡ ⚒ ⚕

For your first election, this guide recommends targeting a 75 percent-win rate, with the other 25 percent spread out among the opposition. That makes it nice and clear who you are going to be victimizing after you've consolidated power. If you are in some backwards country with a two-party state, gift 5 – 7 percent to a write-in candidate. You will be surprised how many people write-in a non-candidate's name. The people don't deserve democracy.

CHAPTER 7

OVERDUE FOR A COUP

"Cruel leaders are replaced only to have new leaders turn cruel."

— CHE GUEVARA, T-SHIRT MASCOT

Welcome to Chapter 7, especially non-readers who decided to skip the messiness that is a democratic election. Isn't it a pain in the ass? All that work, all those backhanded, secretive tactics coupled with the "pretending to care about people" perspective that you have to adopt throughout.

You are a person of action, someone who does what they say, says what they think, and thinks "what the hell is wrong with brute force?" This chapter is for you and your army – and you better have an army.

Despite what Hollywood movies, BBC News Segments, and your crazy revolutionary neighbor who spends his time in the woods would tell you, coups are generally non-violent. There are rarely coups that begin with angry protestors in the streets or rogue government officers locking down the palace. Those scenes from the movie, *Singin' in the Rain* where the protesters led by Gene Kelly rush through the wet streets to overpower the government forces and take back the city are a bit over the top. I know that doesn't seem right, but this author doesn't know enough about the movie to worry about it.

Regardless of the liberal media's depiction, a coup is often necessary when other means won't cut it. Sometimes, you need to take the shortcut to power if you have the means to do so. You will be in good company if you can successfully complete a coup. This includes the likes of Napoleon in France, Ghaddafi in Libya, The Shah of Iran, Saddam Hussein in Iraq, Mobutu Sese Seko in the Congo, and Gene Kelly in the United States.

Fig. 17: Image From The Movie, Singin' In The Rain (1952)

Although it is a shortcut in comparison to "totally legitimate" elections – preparing for and carrying out a coup still unfortunately requires some work if it is to succeed. You will need to get your posse together, plan your takeover, and ensure that it is done as smoothly as possible. This takes some planning.

Setting the Stage – Accrue Your Coup Crew

There are plenty of strong leaders who could not have achieved absolute power without their viziers surrounding them and lifting them up. Think of Hitler and his Kampfbund Leaders during the Beer Hall Putsch, Caligula and his Loyal Bodyguards, Donald Trump and the Proud Boys, Fidel Castro and the Comrades, or Marky Mark and the Funky Bunch.

It is important to have a small cohort of loyalists who not only support your cause but who are also well connected with important sectors of the country. These would be the military (most important), the economy (i.e., the banks), and social aspects (e.g., connections with celebrities, sports stars, behind-the-scenes magic-makers, and Dwayne Johnson, for some reason).

COURT THE CREW – INVEST IN YOUR PEOPLE NOW

Obviously, these people will play their part in your coup. Work with them early on and invest in their future so they will ensure yours in power. After that, who gives a shit?

Start with the bankers. If they are to back you and your army you need to convince them that you will be successful in your takeover of the government. No money, no problems, no coup. Think of it as asking for a loan to buy a house, go to college, or purchase a car. In this case, the interest rate is far lower, and you might actually pay it off in a regular human lifetime.

Next, target the military leaders. You may – and should – already have some of their support because as it was said earlier, you need a goddamn army to make this work. One danger of relying solely on the military is their tendency to show loyalty. They spent their years protecting the current government, and now they must betray them to serve you. Of course, you are the rightful leader of the country, so they should already be on your side, but you must be careful in this assumption.

A recent study found that military academies in countries often facilitated the most effective coups, as they were perfect organizational areas in which military officers can plan them. Take note of this in your lead-up planning to the eventual takeover. Indoctrination ain't just for the kids.

Finally, shop around with your socialites. Refer back to Chapter 5 and subject yourself to some horrible TikTok experiences. Social media has already toppled governments in the Middle East and South America; now it's time for you to utilize it with the help of your crew. Influence extends beyond the politics and economics of your chosen country and so should your hand of power.

POWER BROKER – IF IT AIN'T BROKE, BRIBE IT

Fig. 18: Bribing The Elite Is A Professional, International Sport

The elite are the true brokers of power in most countries today. Think of it this way. Capitalism won out, then sucked everything dry and now it is begging for more. It is the rich cocaine-fueled cousin that you cannot stop hanging out with because he knows where the best parties are in the city. These elites will be the major piece in the coordination of your coup.

Initiating a coup without a critical mass of support from the elites in your country is a recipe for disaster. The failed coup in Turkey in 2016 is a prime example of what not to do when it comes to coups. A cadre of rogue military and political officers attempted to oust the government of Recep Tayyip Erdogan. They failed miserably. A major reason was chaos among their ranks as leaders from the intelligence organization, military, and political officers were not aligned and had not brought in the appropriate elites to help with their scheme.

Brazil presents a wonderful example of the power of bribing the elite; this was not technically a coup as this book defines it, it was more of an impeachment. In 2017, the president, Dilma Rousseff, was removed from office due to corruption. The hilarious part of this removal was that the faction who removed her had nearly 90 percent of their members accused of corruption – many, if not most, were part of the elite class in Brasilia. In fact, the House Speaker at the time, an organized crime boss, was the one who helped remove Ms. Rousseff. Brilliant, Brazil. Just brilliant.

As you can see, the power of the elite extends beyond their monetary value. More often than not, they are either elected to high political office, have political officials in their pocket through donations, or can sponsor extensive media campaigns to make either one of the first two points happen rather quickly.

MARSHALING SUPPORT – CONSENSUS FOR THE DISSENTIOUS

The elite talk to each other at their fancy dinner parties and *Eyes Wide Shut*-style orgies. Yet, they are still widely dispersed. Those that have their first homes in your country are often at their second or third homes somewhere else. Bribing them is one thing but marshaling them to support for your coup is a bit trickier.

Achieving critical mass with your elite backers is necessary to boosting your coup success rate. There is a delicate balance involved in manufacturing popularity with the poor and middle class while ensuring guarantees for the elites. These guarantees usually range from a reduction of taxes (if they were even taxed) to the promise of providing lucrative, monopolized deals, to natural resources or advertising space. There is no shame in declaring your victory at the Pepsi Presents Podium within the Staples Center House. It may sound odd, but it is totally normal to end all of your speeches with "Eat Fresh."

What is most important is that you divide the commitments to the elites in a very careful way. You may be asking, "Why do I need to kowtow to these different rich assholes?" The answer is that a dictator is unfortunately not a king. While you will gain ultimate power over laws, the economy, resources, and everything in between, you still require support from others.

Even a king needed his feudal lords and knights to rein in the serfs and townspeople. If this author knew a way to control the world without anyone's help, it would have been done already. That is not the case. Your best bet is to cater to the elite in these ways, then a coup will help you get there more quickly. It will also help you avoid needing the support of other 95 percent of the population.

CHAPTER 8

CONGRATULATIONS, GREAT LEADER

"The truth is that men nowadays are tired of liberty"

— BENITO MUSSOLINI, FAMOUS PASTA DISH

Fig. 19: Victory! Throw Your Hands Up In The Air, Like You Just Don't Care About Your People

You did it! You overcame all the obstacles – be they democratic processes, human opponents, or the troll's riddles to cross the bridge of leadership. You have won the adoration of the crowd or instituted a healthy amount of fear in the crowd and reached the top of the slippery ladder. Now it is time to pour hot oil down the ladder, dismantle it, and burn it. Time to begin your reign of terror. It is time to help those who helped you and punish those who didn't. And don't forget to punish those who you just don't like for personal, political, or economic reasons. Punish them all. Get it out early in your reign.

⊕ ✠ ⚡ ☫ ☭

FIRST THINGS FIRST – DISMANTLE DEMOCRACY

If you achieved your win through a coup, then you can probably skip this section. You took a nice shortcut around democracy to get here. Congratulations.

For the rest of you, let's get working on removing the mechanisms that helped you and your cronies gain power. They won't be needed anymore.

Wow, can you believe how much voter fraud occurred during the election? Neither can I, but it is a worthy argument to not only gain support for your win, but also to target the process with falsehoods and questions. As was discussed in an earlier chapter, questioning the potential for voter fraud is projection. Why do you ask? Well first off, you shouldn't be asking questions, but as a freebie, it is a good way to highlight the strength of your win without outwardly showing that you won through less than legal means.

Now it is time to question the legitimacy of the entire democratic process. You may have won victory through it entirely legitimately, but your opponents tried their darnedest to thwart you by cheating, so the whole process is dubious, nonetheless. So, democracy is a sham and while you figured out how to exploit it, it is now your goal to explain how it is a horrible way to elect leaders and/or choose positions for the community, region, or country to take. You need to target the legitimacy and efficacy of the democratic process and discuss how useless it is or – even better – how it can be stolen by the wrong folks (the irony is not lost on this author, and it shouldn't be lost on you). There are a few quick ways to destroy the way that normal people view democracy. You should utilize all of them in your quest.

ADVERTISEMENTS

Hooray for Capitalism yet again! In today's world, you have plenty of advertising avenues through which to share your message with the people.

TELEVISION

You can't believe everything you see on television, right? Wrong! Of course, you can, and your people will believe whatever you put on there. Television is usually a prime candidate for, well, candidates promoting themselves. You are no longer burdened by candidacy. And you will never be burdened by it again. You do not have to spend much money in this sphere but given that the older generations who aren't sharing Facebook memes are still kicking, you will want to cater to them for now. It is probably best to copy the ads of local used car dealers. They tend to make the most of a low budget and have charismatic idiots willing to debase themselves for a quick buck.

PAMPHLETS

No need to throw these out from a plane anymore, but they can still come in handy. It is best to distribute them at doctor's offices, abortion clinics, and multi-level marketing scheme meetings. All of these prey on the sick, vulnerable, and idiotic. Keep it short and simple, just what the people like. Take historical democracy out of context. For instance, democracy in 300 A.D. led to the fall of the Roman Empire, etc. None of that last sentence is correct, but it doesn't matter as long as it *sounds* correct and, in a pamphlet, it will do: I mean, it's printed on glossy paper so it can't be a lie.

Social Media

Let's be honest, the first two options are just paying lip service. This is the king and queen of advertisement, propaganda, and for some reason, great recipes for a slow cooker. Embrace the memes; memes are your lifeblood in this area. You need to avoid being connected to any of them. In fact, never connect yourself to anything now that you are leader of the country for life.

There are plenty of good meme templates on the internet to share with your public. They have the shelf life of a gnat though, so be careful which ones you use. Have your subordinates share these memes across social media platforms – Instagram, TikTok, and Facebook. Facebook is your best option to corral the Boomer generation. They love a good meme as it equates to research these days. Therefore, "research" says that democracy is broken and causes more problems than it solves. You have now solved the problem with your reign.

Fig. 20: Grandma Supporting the Cause Through Social Media Memes

Politics

Wait, you still have to deal with this crap? You won and you are leader – hopefully for life. These people are now under your control, right? Well, buddy, you still have to deal with the various idiots in the parliament or congress in your country. It might be more of a formality, but it is unfortunately a necessary part of your first year or two in office.

YOUR PARTY IS NOW "THE PARTY"

It is necessary to work with your party to help pass laws that deepen your control over the government, economy, and country. Remember that you won under one of the party labels, so stick with them early on. Utilize your "party" (it's in quotes because eventually you will be the only thing that matters) to push out new laws and updates to current laws that help consolidate your power, remove freedoms, and target your opponents.

The Party is now the first descriptor in your identity and those of everyone that you now lord it over. Everything else is secondary to the Party now. All actions taken by your people must be questioned with regard to how it helps the Party. The Party comes before your gods, your job, your family, and your friends.

JUDGE, JURY, EXECUTIONER

Your first actions for the Party should be ramming through as many judges as possible across local, state, province, and national arenas. The candidates don't even have to be qualified – sycophants, loyalists, your nephew who is a failure at everything he does – the list goes on and on. They will be key to carrying out your new laws and handing down extremely harsh punishments to your opponents and detractors. Sorry, Billy, but the tariff for jaywalking in Milwaukee is now life imprisonment. Could be worse, Sally is going to be executed for littering. Cleanliness is a strong pillar in your new government.

Installing your loyalist judges is a helpful way to begin arresting, trying, and jailing your political opponents. They will also be essential as you begin to roll back freedoms and suspend rights – you may announce these suspensions as "temporary" (wink wink).

Fig. 21: Off to Jail for Little Timmy

SUSPENSION TIME – YOU HAVE THE RIGHT TO REMOVE ALL RIGHTS

Let's go through some of the major freedoms and rights that you can begin to roll back. You will want to choose your words carefully (or don't mention them at all) as you start removing these rights. You don't want to do them all at once, which could cause an unnecessary stir early in your reign. Slow and steady wins the race and ensures no one else crosses the finish line ever again. Remember, authoritarianism is a marathon, not a sprint.

- *Speech.* It is important that we don't allow people to disseminate lies about the regime.
- *Independent Media.* According to this report you just made up, the rest of the media is lying and cannot be trusted to continue to exist.
- *Assembly.* Thugs are getting together and organizing flash mobs, a danger to society.
- *Internet Access.* Your kids are looking at porn, let's curtail that pernicious threat.
- *Life.* Don't we have too many people already? Overpopulation is not good for the economy.
- *Liberty.* Freedom means that people you don't like also have that freedom; why not remove it and ensure your enemies aren't free?

- *Happiness.* Get angry, and if you are already angry, make others angry at the world. Complacency is the devil's work.

⊕ ✠ ✨ ☭ ☭

AWARD YOUR LOYALISTS

Now it's time to reward your loyal supporters who stuck with you throughout the campaign trail, intimidated voters, attacked your opponents, and sprinkled fraud wherever they went.

Cabinet positions for all! Be sure to install your family members in close positions and advisory roles. Sure, none of them are qualified. In fact, one of your brothers has a massive drug addiction, your other brother has an IQ in the single digits, and your younger sister eats babies. Either way, those are perfect qualifications for Secretary of State, Education Administrator, and Chief of Staff. You can decide who belongs in which role by tossing a coin.

Fig. 22: Nincompoop Nepotism

Your positions don't have to be one-for-one either! Loyalists can hold multiple positions or you can simply give them some generic advisory role where they sit on the decision boards across arenas of governance.

For those grunt workers that helped you, it is always good to setup a slush fund (more on that shortly) to provide periodic kickbacks to the intermediaries of the party. Establishing a system of bribery and corruption ensures you keep a cadre of happy followers to do your bidding and police the rest of your people. But be careful; if you give a mouse a cookie, it is going to ask for milk. When it does, it's time to kill the mouse. Fear is still the ultimate motivator.

PAYDAY – RAIDING THE GOVERNMENT COFFERS

It is time to set up your kleptocracy! As newly appointed leader, embezzlement and thievery are now state-sanctioned. Let's be honest, those hard-earned dollars would look so much nicer in a Swiss bank account rather than languishing in your country's dusty coffers.

Of course, you don't want to keep all your money in Geneva. Spread the wealth around. Seychelles, Belgium, Panama, the Caribbean are all great places to have a few extra accounts. This will come in handy later if conniving international organizations try to freeze and/or seize your assets.

The financial investigators are often smarter than they look so you will need to get clever with your funds. It is good to constantly move your money around through convoluted transactions. No need to get bogged down in the details here, there are plenty of corrupt bankers who will be more than happy to do the heavy financial lifting. Deutsche Bank has a long, storied history and experience in this regard. If you want to go even a step further, take a page from former Ukrainian Prime Minister. Mr. Pavlo Lazarenko, who went ahead and bought his own bank to launder funds through – now that is thinking outside the box, or the bank.

Don't forget to lawyer up. Next to the bloodsucking bankers, lawyers are an autocrat's best friend when it comes to embezzlement. Your army of lawyers can help you make sure that any potential seizure or forfeiture is tied up in legal battles for years. The lawyers for Ferdinand Marcos of the Philippines were able to tie up $365 million in litigation for over twelve years. Money buys time: time you may need to escape or find clever ways to move your money around before it is seized.

If you play your credit cards right, you can enjoy many decades of extreme wealth, financial security, a constant slush fund for bribery, and a level of luxury usually reserved for royalty.

THE ALL-SEEING EYE

Sauron is a great case of promoting a strong surveillance state to keep his people under control. Although, he did let two little people get by him right under his nose. Instead, take a page from Xi Jinping, or as he loves to be known, Winnie the Pooh. He has far more support than just a bunch of blinded white guys.

Winnie the Watcher has created a comprehensive surveillance apparatus that spans over a billion subjects. The government has managed to utilize the internet to provide all social services to its people, requiring them to rely on it to live and function.

Fig. 23: Winnie Loves Playing I-Spy

Smart move as Winnie's government has also managed to control all aspects of it through devices like "The Great Firewall of China," blocking any remotely bad opinions about the government. He also has a well-oiled state television and news media (e.g., CCTV), and a brilliant new method of instituting "social credits" that allow the good citizens more access to goods and services within the country. The next chapter will delve more deeply into this so you are prepared to move toward the middle years of your rule.

Hopefully, you have a semi-functional intelligence service already working within the country. Although their original tasks may have been to find terrorists, counteract adversaries and propaganda, you can now utilize their systems to track your citizens. It is imperative that you invest additional funds into building your surveillance state as soon as possible. You don't want all your hard work gaining power to be ruined by a couple of filthy hobbits.

From Civil Society To Chaos Society

For those of you who didn't study politics and government, the definition of civil society is simply a community of people that share common interests and collective activity in service of the country. For you, civil society is a collective danger to your rule. It must be divided and exploited.

Begin your ruthless rule of law by repressing the various grass roots organizations rampant in your country. These groups of young, college-educated, and politically active people present a danger to your power. If you tolerate their talk of freedoms, understanding of the intricacies of government, and free time, they can make life far too difficult for you and your fledgling rule.

Haiti presents a lovely case study for how to accomplish this feat. In 1992, following the downfall of Francois Duvalier this kind of repression worked toward destroying all forms of independent association in the country, whether it was political organizations, religious bake offs, atheist bake offs, bakery religion offs, kid's birthday parties, symposiums, grassroots groups, college keggers, or whatever.

Silence is golden. So put your team to work in order to silence as many of the youth as you can. The youth is a big part of civil society, and they will continue to be a thorn in your side throughout your lifelong rule. The next chapter will discuss additional tactics to ensure a disabled, weakened society filled with infighting. Make them fight each other so they don't get together and try to fight you.

Authoritarian Claus Is Coming To Town

Remember the Blame Game wheel during your campaign? Well, it is time to dust off that wheel – although shame on you for not keeping it in pristine condition. Cleanliness is next to godliness, and you are basically God now.

It is time to start making lists of your opponents, potential enemies (whether real or imagined – usually imagined), and prominent figures within each of the Blame Game categories. Don't forget to check your lists twice and ensure that everyone on it has most likely been naughty.

Utilize your burgeoning surveillance state to begin monitoring these people, who they meet with, and especially anything they talk about in person, on the phone, or in social media. You must watch them at all times, even when they are sleeping, and you better believe you know when they are awake.

At this early stage of your rule, nothing more than monitoring and recording these people is needed. The data will come in handy later on as you begin to cull the herd and exercise a more iron-fisted rule over your people. At this stage, you are in Boy Scout mode – always be prepared.

Your First Speech

It is time to give your first official speech to the people. This will help you outline your agenda, provide "dog whistle" language to your loyal supports, communicate veiled threats to your opponents, showcase your strength and leadership, and babble on and on about whatever crazy, off-the-wall, bigoted, evil things you want to get off your chest without any more repercussions.

Key things to mention in your speech should be words like "citizen," "flag," "a new dawn," "strength," "crime," "America (either for it if you are American, or against it if you are literally any other country), "military," "economy," and "authority." These are just a few examples, but the theme must be strength and overt nationalism. Most of the people will be your supporters, so hype them up and get them riled up. You will want to continue to go back to this language in subsequent speeches, particularly during low points in your rule [more on that in the next Chapter 9].

Your Inaugural Speech: A Brief Template

Dear Citizens of [Your Country], Dear Friends!

Today, I appeal to you who have entrusted me with the highest office in our country. It is time for us to come together and rebuild our country, restoring its promise for all of our people – at least for all of the people who are patriotic, deserving workers who fully understand the responsibilities that come with the privilege of being a citizen here.

Every four years, we gather on these steps to carry out the orderly and peaceful transfer of power. Too often, this process has been abused by crooked politicians who have stolen elections from the rightful choices of you the people. We must fix the broken democratic process to ensure the correct result in future.

Today's ceremony, however, has very special meaning, because today we are not merely transferring power from one administration to another, or from one party to another, but we are transferring power from our capital, and giving it back to you, the people (hold for laughs).

Our nation has suffered at the hands of drugs, crime, that strange mist that has been turning people inside out, poverty, and loss of factories. Netflix has been cancelling our favorite shows too early, we have a failing education system, a never-ending flow of hard seltzers, and roving gangs of liberals.

We must stand together and rise together to bring our country back to greatness. Our new national pride will stir our souls, lift our sights, fill up our beers, and heal our divisions. It's time to remember that old wisdom our soldiers will never forget, whether you are white, or Caucasian, or Christian, or Rich [Note: replace these with whatever the majority group is in your country].

We all enjoy the same glorious rights, and we all salute the same, great [Your Country] flag. No matter who we are, we look up at the same night sky, fill our hearts with the same dreams of world domination, and are infused with the generational wealth we have coasted through life on.

So to all my Citizens, in every city near and far, from every humble worker's hut to every penthouse, from mountain to mountain, from our great [additional national geography]. You will never be ignored again. We will make our country strong again. We will certainly not ignore our detractors. God bless you and thank you.

LOOKING TO THE FUTURE: YOUR LONG-TERM AGENDA

You are starting to settle into your new reign, you've laid out your agenda, begun to eliminate opponents, rolled back rights, and stripped freedoms. Now it is time to look out toward the horizon. Remember, you are going to be ruler for life. Once you have snuffed out any possibility of being removed from power (at least legally), you need to start thinking of how about spend your days.

Sure, removing your opponents and people you don't like is fun, but, sooner or later, you run out of a constant supply of fodder. Sure, spending your days relaxing and enjoying a life of luxury courtesy of your country's resources is wonderful, but it can get dull.

The country is your oyster, and you are only limited by your imagination. Let's discuss a few activities and projects with which you may want to consider filling your days of authoritarian bliss.

Sell Assets to China

This is a very popular activity today, especially across the African continent. China has become Daddy Warbucks in Africa over the last couple of decades. They are now the top lender to the continent and the leading lender to 32 countries totaling tens of billions of dollars. They clearly have no ulterior motive in this. They are just generous guys.

There are a couple of benefits to pursuing this project. For one, it is pretty darn easy to do. And who doesn't like an easy way to get a few extra *yuan* in their pocket. As your taste for luxury expands to a near insatiable level, you will need to continue to fund your hedonism. The government coffers don't last forever without some money coming into the country. Now, you could try to build up a vibrant economy and export goods or services, but honestly that is a drag and it might give your subjects more autonomy – much better simply to sell irreplaceable government assets to China.

A second benefit is that you can easily combine this project with various other activities. It can even help fund your unjust wars, collection of art for money laundering, or buildings in other countries to further showcase your insane wealth.

But what exactly are these assets you should sell? Land (or water) rights are the most precious assets you have at your disposable. If your country has a coast, you have a good chance of selling those maritime rights for offshore drilling or aggressive fishing and dredging. Mineral rights are another major asset that can garner you a hefty payday. Careful with these as you may want to have a few in your back pocket in case you need a quick influx of cash to fund a war or quell internal strife. Finally, while not as exciting to your Chinese buyers as geographic rights, selling the rights to your government buildings is another way to bring in some extra dollars. Feel free to sell the buildings that once housed your legislature, libraries, and other civil service buildings – you will not need those for much longer anyhow.

Start A Disinformation Campaign

For the computer nerds, software geeks, and internet trolls, this is an exceedingly fun project to take on during your rule. Who wouldn't want to have an army of hackers, internet jackasses, and meme connoisseurs doing their bidding and ruining the lives of random strangers who made you angry in the YouTube comments of your campaign videos?

There are several benefits to adding this to your long-term project list. First, it makes it easy and fun to attack or de-stabilize your global adversaries. Once you have defeated your enemies within your country, you are going to want to harass your enemies abroad. A disinformation campaign is much cheaper than starting a full-blown war against another enemy country. In addition, it makes it easier to hide your evidence, claim innocence, and keep those pesky international organizations like the United Nations, NATO, or Human Rights Watch off your back.

Another benefit of this campaign is that it can always be turned inward to promote misinformation or disinformation against your internal opponents – they tend to pop up over the years (sometimes fueled by enemy countries or intelligence agencies). When they do pop up, you will have a great apparatus with which to quickly whack them back down and keep your people in line with a constant stream of online propaganda.

Creating a disinformation army is easier than it may seem. Russia provides the most successful example with their "Internet Research Agency." This Russian troll farm has managed to wreak disinformative havoc across Eastern Europe, Western Europe, and the United States. You'll want to start recruiting and training your troll army as soon as you can. Your best places to find these reprobates are Reddit, 4chan, IT departments, High Schools, and Middle Schools (those kids are brutally deranged). You'll want to work with your intelligence agencies to help with messaging that your trolls can convert to Facebook memes, guerilla-style commenting across message boards and social media websites, and hundreds of fake or bot accounts to help divide and enrage the citizens of other countries. Make the braindead social media addicts in other countries work for you. See the last 10 years of the United States' political climate for a near flawless example of the success of a disinformation campaign.

Once you get your troll farm blasting out propaganda at a speedy clip, all you have to do is sit back, relax, and watch your enemies slowly destroy themselves from the inside out. This is all over a bunch of memes. We are doomed as a species. Might as well lean into it.

START A GENOCIDE (NOT RECOMMENDED)

Some genocides are planned, and some come out more organically. It is important to mention this activity as it can help you get rid of opponents or undesirables, but the risk is often much greater than the reward.

The violent removal of a singular group of people based on their shared identity is a mindset that often gets dictators in trouble. There are certainly some benefits to this if you really need to remove this group due to their unified opposition to your rule. It is also often a quick – albeit dirty – way to please your supporters.

These benefits are far outweighed by the problems that arise when undertaking a genocide. First, it brings far too much attention to you from outside the country. No matter how hard you try, word will eventually get out. Unless you are China and have the commercial power to drown out any humanitarian complaints, then you are going to run into obstacles. For instance, a genocide is a quick ticket to a trial at the Hague. Although there are ways out of that [more on that later].

Similarly, sanctions can be enforced by other countries and international organizations. This is an even bigger pain in the ass as you may lose access to your favorite American DVDs, caviar, champagne, Snuggies, concerts from famous singers like Mariah Carey (who once performed for Muammar Gaddafi), and other luxury goods. While sanctions often hurt a country's citizens more than they do the leader, do you want to risk missing out on the next Marvel movie release? Is wiping out your opponents worth not having Apple TV+?

Finally, genocide can take a toll on your funds and your people who have to carry it out. Let's face it, no matter what method you do, it's going to either cost plenty of money and supplies or cost a hefty contribution of manpower.

INCREASE YOUR NUMBER OF LABOR CAMPS

A healthy alternative to genocide is to build forced labor camps across your country. In this way, you can avoid the undue attention that mass killings bring upon you. At the same time, you create a mechanism of free labor with which to: mine resources; reeducate political opponents; break stones; create and sell Nike merchandise. It also allows you to provide any number of factory-produced goods to sell on the global free market. Thank god for capitalism.

You will have to invest a bit of money into your camps, but it will provide a greater return down the line. You can easily scale up your chosen model of labor camp whenever you want – or need – to imprison more people and make more money. It is usually good to take a percentage of a family and threaten the others with forced labor, thus keeping your citizens in line and under your power.

Fig. 24: Forced Labor – A Hallowed Tradition

There are plenty of good labor camp models from which to choose. You will want to place your camps in a remote part of your country – usually hidden in mountains, as this will ensure enemy satellites have trouble detecting them. There are the more traditional models popularized in Russia and North Korea – barbed wire fences, ominous watchtowers, squat, concrete buildings. Don't feel obliged to keep it traditional though. It is the 21st century after all. Add some color to your buildings. Perhaps get a famous graffiti artist to help out - Banksy may be available.

You may want to have the camp in a more enclosed model, like an Amazon Fulfillment Center. This allows you to post up motivational banners and posters to help encourage your slaves. A few examples you may want to integrate into your camp motivational banners:

"When You're Here, You're Family"

"Nothing is Ever Achieved Without Some Pain and Work"

"Slave Less, Smile More"

"Have It Your Way (As long As It's Our Way)"

"It Could be Worse; This Could be an Applebee's"

"Slave, Laugh, Love"

"Choose a Job You Love, and You Will Never Have to Work a Day In Your Life"

The possibilities truly are endless, just like the labor available from your camps.

START A PROXY WAR

You may be wondering why such a specific war. Wouldn't any old type of war work for your hobby? Wrong. Traditional, all-out wars are costly in terms of time, manpower, and funds. Unless you are planning to fully take over the country (and are able to) and are going to gain more resources from it, then a fully-fledged war is a poor idea.

On the other hand, starting a proxy war can be a fun way to pass the time at a lower cost to you. Superpowers of the past like the United States and the Soviet Union had an absolute blast funding different warlords, guerrilla groups, and corrupt governments with money, guns, and intelligence.

Proxy wars can provide great benefits to you and keep you occupied with how the conflicts unfold. You can make a good amount of money by selling arms, military training, or other material needs to the belligerents. Remember, all your projects should attempt to bring in more money rather than spending it. Always spend it on yourself; you deserve it.

Another great benefit is all the fun messiness that can come out of proxy wars, like child soldiers – they are so cute with their little hats and rifles! In addition, you can have hilariously ironic names for the guerrilla fighters such as:

- *Revolutionary United Front* - Sierra Leone
- *Coalition of Patriots for Change* - Central African Republic
- *Revolutionary Left Movement* - Chile
- *Lord's Resistance Army* - Uganda
- *The Judean People's Front* - Judea
- *The People's Front of Judea* - Judea

Latin America and Africa do have the monopoly on great guerrilla movement names.

Be careful to avoid sponsoring guerrilla forces that are too close to your own country. You don't want that messiness to spill over into your own borders. Don't shit where you eat.

START A EUGENICS PROGRAM

Speaking of pooping where you eat – kids. You have probably been in a situation like this before. You are out at the local Despot Depot to buy some novelty Stalin bobbleheads and all of the sudden a whirling mass of tiny people run past you knocking all the Trump Clapping Monkeys onto the ground. A frazzled parent slowly walks past talking on their cell phone without a care in the world. You don't have to deal with that anymore.

Eugenics is a common term for "selective breeding." The principle has been around since 300-400 B.C. Although the original principle was to create a genetically superior species, that has proven to not be the case. Any success in that field eventually leads to genetic similarities and your population may start looking like Alabama. On the other hand, you can institute draconian measures to prevent certain people you deem unfit from producing offspring. These could be your opponents, people unfit to raise children, inbreeders, deviants, reality TV families, criminals, and YouTube personalities.

Be careful as you roll out your program. People will start to notice. You also want to ensure that those who you target do not overlap with any of your own supporters. Still, a eugenics program is a bit more fun than just instituting a "No Kids" policy at public places.

INVEST IN LARGE PUBLIC WORKS PROJECTS

Just kidding! Why would you be stupid enough to waste your hard stolen money on your people? Sure, they may have contributed to it through political support or paying their taxes, but is that really enough to warrant a new water desalination plant?

Now, you may want to put a twist on this activity in that you can sell the rights to the project to an outside bidder (e.g., China, United States). These outside bidders can provide you with a healthy number of bribes and kickbacks while cutting corners on every aspect of the project. For instance:

- *New Roads.* Does that interstate need guardrails? Probably not, the drivers just need to be careful.
- *New Stadiums.* Sure, the national soccer team is full of drunks, disabled, and MLS players, but they deserve a new $1.2 billion dollar stadium. OK, so the new stadium might not have the appropriate supports in place for the fans, but what would a few hundred deaths in a collapse matter in the grand scheme of things?
- *New Parks.* Astro turf is just as good as real grass, plus it's a great way to sprinkle in some new statues of you for your subjects to gaze upon and despair.
- *New Airports.* Bring in the tourists and make a ton of money off the terminal food stalls and Hudson Newsstands. Don't worry that the air traffic control tower is leaning that far to one side; the pilots will figure it out.

Fig. 25: Cutting The Ribbon On Your New Country's Rolling Skating Rink

You won't have to bother with any maintenance for these projects after they are complete either. You can promise improvements as part of your ever-growing list that you provide in your speeches that you will never follow-through on for the country.

Sponsor Terrorism

This is another cheap way to avoid costly wars while still ensuring you create chaos for your global foes. It might seem dangerous to tangle with terrorists given that they have such a bad reputation, but that is mostly their lack of proper marketing. You can funnel your funds through any number of ways that the author hopes you have set up, as discussed earlier. Hopefully you can help these groups hire a well-known marketing firm to polish their image like a Burston-Marsteller, an Ogilvy, a PwC, or Fox News.

Terrorists often come much cheaper than sponsoring whole proxy wars and guerrilla armies too. They are the Super Saver Deal for sowing global chaos. Most of the time, when they are successful, they die, thus cleaning up any paper trail pretty quickly and easily for you. An added bonus is the affected country often implements additional draconian security measures on its own citizens rather than trying to combat the funding mechanisms. You can recline in your chair as you watch foreigners be humiliated in TSA lines thousands of miles away. Although more TSA staffers can breed more dictators, as discussed in an earlier chapter. It's a risk worth taking though; they might create some new friends for you at the dictator's BBQ in the future. Soon you'll be able to have an entire dictator intramural softball league!

COZY UP WITH THE CIA

Last, but certainly not least is working with the Central Intelligence Agency (CIA). They are willing to throw any amount of funding directly at you – often in heavy bags of cash as they did with the former leader of Afghanistan, Hamid Karzai.

All they usually want in exchange is a few bits of intelligence about terrorism (hey, you might be able to help with that!), safe passage for activities in neighboring countries (such as airport use for special forces or arms smuggling), or to help you quash leftist and communist guerilla groups.

Of course, the CIA can be a double-edged sword, so you have to keep on your toes when dealing with them. They can be a fickle bunch that may be willing to supply your opponents if the U.S. administration changes or if they can get a better deal with your opposition leader (he might have one of those 15 percent coupons that come in the mail from companies like Bed, Bath and Beyond).

These are just a few examples of hobbies you can pursue throughout your rule. The sky is the limit when it comes to these types of projects and activities, you can do multiple ones at a time, mix and match, or put your own special twist on them. Nothing can stop you, given a deep cache of government funds, an insatiable need for more, and the thin line between your genius and insanity. Get designing and get planning.

CHAPTER 9

ABSOLUTE POWER: HOLD ON TIGHTLY

"It's worth remembering that it is often the small steps, not the giant leaps, that bring about the most lasting change."

— QUEEN ELIZABETH II, MONARCHICAL CYBORG

Winning or rigging an election is the relatively easy part of your rule. Now you have the next half a century (fingers crossed) or more to hold onto power. You need to ensure that you can do everything to your heart and wallet's desire. You will encounter many different challenges and challengers to your reign.

You need to prepare yourself for these obstacles. This chapter is dedicated to ensuring you are able to hold on to your newfound power for many, many years. Like the New England Patriots football team, we want to keep you at the top of your game and ensure your dynasty.

Fig. 26: Through Demagoguery And Deflation, Tom Brady Sustained Absolute Power Over The NFL For 20+ Years

Leveraging the lessons from the great authoritarians who have managed to hold on for multiple decades – such as the Kim Dynasty, Big, Bad, Vlad Putin, Robert Mugabe, and many more – you will be ready for anything that is thrown (like a grenade, a shoe, or a civil lawsuit) your way. This is where we separate the boys from the autocrats.

⊕ ✠ ϟ ࿕ ☭

DADDY DICTATOR – THE ULTIMATE PROTECTOR

There is a well-known instinct for most people to seek protection from a strong, fatherly figure (sorry ladies, although there is a maternal Margaret Thatcher-like role you can aim for, too). This is especially prevalent in the less-educated populace, which, as discussed, is a pretty big majority of the global population.

Here is a quick science lesson. Utilize the concept of science loosely as you don't want to rely on it too much as it can lead to free thinking. No one wants free thinkers roaming around their country. Tens of thousands of years ago, our ancestors were bonded to powerful leaders. In terms of evolution, the people who stuck with the most powerful leader were likely to survive the harsh environment. That instinct was passed along and is still well entrenched in the reptilian brains of humans today. Thus, it is easy for you to exploit and capitalize on it to sustain your power for many years to come. Darwinian dictatorship if you will.

This level of power worship can also be attributed to certain cultures. This is especially true in Asia where respect for leaders is such a cultural norm, it is virtually a requirement. In the West, children tend to throw their useless grandparents in prison or maybe nursing homes: no real difference. In the East, grandparents are taken care of throughout their life in the homes of their children and grandchildren. Thus in Asia, whether you are the local schoolteacher or Kim Jon Un, the ultimate schoolteacher, you must be respected.

The lesson here is to portray yourself as the fatherly figure throughout your rule. You are the protector of the country and the people. You let them sit on your lap and read them stories about the evils of free thought and unions. You go outside and play catch with them. Not to catch the baseball, but to catch the underground opposition supporter. A few other examples that work:

UNCLE JOE

This was a term that the allies used for good Ol' Joseph Stalin during World War II. Every child loves a good uncle; he gives them extra presents during the holidays, takes them to the park, and sneaks them sips of whiskey when they are having a bad day at elementary school. Everyone respects uncles, whether or not they are drunk at Thanksgiving. An uncle presents a great "father" figure without any of the promises or responsibilities that come with being an actual father.

THE GODFATHER

Mario Puzo's notorious family of mafiosos gave us the orange-loving Marlon Brando. He showed that the love of a godfather is often a symbol of fear. Ruthlessness, terror, and unintelligible mumbling provides a great set of characteristics you can embody as the godfather of your nation. The first two are fairly self-explanatory – terror and ruthlessness should be key pillars of your rule regardless of your adopted title. Unintelligible mumbling is a dark horse characteristic as you can announce edits, decrees, and removals of freedoms without anyone knowing during the initial announcement. In addition, at some point you can have your Chief of Staff shut the doors in the face of a leader just like the movie. Always take the chance to recreate iconic movie scenes during your reign. It is all about the little things in life.

Mrs. Doubtfire

You may be wondering how a voice actor wearing a bodysuit to play a British nanny can help you in sustaining power. Well, that is a good question. First, it certainly sows confusion among your people – and among readers of this guide. Confusion is a great way to prevent or at the very least delay anger, so jot that down. Euphegenia Doubtfire is a prime example of how far fathers will go – the extra kilometer if you will – for their children. Now, maybe you don't go to the next regional conference in a dress, but don't rule it out. The theme here is that you are willing to do whatever it takes to help your people. Even if that is all a lie, which it is, it is all about image.

The God, and the Father

No need to stop at being a fatherly figure. Go for the full god complex. This has worked for the likes of Mussolini, Kim Jong-Il, and Donald Trump. All have claimed themselves either to be a god or to be equal to the creator. If you ran your campaign on a religious pillar, or, even better, you took over a predominantly religious country, you are already in a prime position for this role.

For example, Mussolini instituted a fascist religion that required complete belief in "Il Duce," the revolution, and the government. This requires a hefty investment in indoctrination of the younger generation in your country, but you will want to do that regardless. The added benefit of this image is that you can claim wildly bizarre miracles [more on that next chapter] to further justify yourself as a god who will protect the fatherland (lots of misogynistic aspects here, huh?). This also allows you to keep the religious elite under your control by forcing them to change their sermons to include you and help push your messages and strengthen your rule for years to come. And for those who resist this suggestion, there is plenty of room in the labor camps.

Hearts and Minds

Psychological operations are a fun little activity to use against your enemies, but they are also useful for controlling your citizenry in order to hold on to power. The intelligence community has made leaps and strides in perfecting many ways of torturing people utilizing psychological techniques and methods. However, there are plenty of tactics that are available to address whatever they deem fit. You can win and hold the hearts and minds of your people, whether they like it or not.

Propaganda

This has been discussed in various ways throughout this guide, but it is important to take a closer look at it now as you seek to sustain power. If you chose to build a disinformation army, then you are already a step ahead of the game.

Whatever media outlet you utilize to propagate your propaganda – if not all of them, since you own them all – be sure to base it on three key principles:

1. Constant

Your propaganda must be distributed at a frequency that rivals Bed, Bath, and Beyond coupons or deals on cell phone plans. A continuous push of your tailored messages will ensure that your citizens are bombarded by them and will have no reason to stray away from your "benevolent" rule (be sure to use the word "benevolent" a lot in your messaging).

2. CONSISTENT

Well, consistency is in the eye of the beholder, and you are the only one that holds everything. Of course, you aren't going to have the same message across multiple decades; the key is to keep the overall messaging the same. People love consistency and hate change, so utilize the same format on your posters, reuse memes, and repurpose slogans without changing too much. De Beers has used "A Diamond is Forever" for 73 years and still is successfully selling those magic beans to people. Don't "Think Different," think "Mostly the Same."

3. CONFUSING

Keep your propaganda hard to fully pin down. Historically, people have struggled to differentiate propaganda from other types of biased persuasion. Is a historical documentary on your country propaganda? (Subtext: no.) Is Fox News propaganda? (Subtext: yes.) Is Thomas the Tank Engine propaganda? (Subtext: yes.) Is that vaguely Cold War-esque military poster propaganda? (Subtext: the jury is still out). Is the Pledge of Allegiance propaganda? (Subtext: Oh, yes.) You should get the idea by now; confuse the populace and ensure you can push out your propaganda without any question. Project the questions onto others.

⊕ ✠ ✻ ☬ ☭

DEMORALIZATION

This should be fairly easy these days given that most people are demoralized with the whole state of the world. Even so, you should plan to erode your opponents' morale further through forced intimidation, incapacitation, and jailing. The key here is to ensure that anyone who even begins to mention the decaying structure of your rule, government, or infrastructure is immediately beaten down mentally. They need to know there is nothing they can do to better their situation except put their hopes in you. Better than demoralization is re-moralization, where you push them to be optimistic about opportunities that will never come. It is a bit like kicking the can down the road, but you will be surprised how far you can kick a can when you have a giant, authoritarian boot.

FALSE FLAG OPERATIONS

Another fun activity to have your loyalists engage in to benefit your propaganda. A relatively new tactic in the grand scheme of authoritarianism, false flagging began in the 16th century to misrepresent the motives of the opponents. Although it requires a bit of physical warfare to commit to the operation – such as airfare or land operations – it all contributes to the overall level of psychological control you can impose on your citizens.

With false flag operations, you can blame everyone and every country at your disposal to rile up your citizens, put them on high alert to protect your kingdom, and, as a bonus, get them to focus their anger on another group of people. It is always a good time to break out your Blame Game wheel!

KNOW YOUR MINERAL RIGHTS (TO THE TUNE OF KOKOMO)

> Manganese, and Nestle, ooh I want to take me
> Zambia, Botswana, come on pretty mama
> Zimbabwe and Beryl
> Baby why don't we go
> Ooh I wanna take you down to the Congo
> We'll mine it fast
> And then we'll make some dough

> That's where we want to go
> Way down in the Congo

The Beach Boys were right when they sang that song. It is common knowledge that they were talking about dominating your country through owning and selling out your mineral assets to the highest bidder. As discussed in the previous chapter, this is a solid avenue for selling assets to China and generating additional funds for your coffers. However, you need to be careful with giving too much of your mine ownership away too fast.

Rare earth minerals have become increasingly important in the last few years. The world requires more of them to create: semiconductors and computer chips for use in military applications (e.g., drones, aircraft radar alignment, Call of Duty, PlayStation games); civilian applications (e.g., 3D porn, whatever the hell Meta is under Facebook, and more porn); and socially useful applications (e.g., N/A). If you do not have access to these minerals, probably best to skip this section, as you will be angry at what you could have and want to launch an invasion – just remember that you are still special in your own way. Anyway, this section is nearly over, so here you are.

Et Tu, Brute?

Nothing can ruin your extended time at the top of the mountain than an assassination. What a pain in the back. A mortally-wounding one at that. Plenty of great leaders had their rule tragically cut short by assassinations – often by their closest advisors and friends.

Benito Mussolini. The OG of modern fascism and ruler of Italy, along with his mistress, Clara Petacci, was shot while trying to escape to Switzerland. Italian partisans had once been loyal to "Il Duce" (i.e., The Duke – like John Wayne). These partisans were once his loyal guards at the border, but unfortunately, to Il Duce's surprise, they changed sides to the Allies. Their bodies were hung upside down in Milan for all to ridicule. Talk about your whole world turning upside, literally.

Jesus Christ. One of the original benevolent leaders, who was betrayed by Judas Iscariot. While Jesus was not technically "assassinated," it is worth mentioning here. Thirty pieces of silver is all it took to rat out the guy, so a bit more expensive than a U.S congressperson in today's dollars. On the bright side, Judas has his name forever remembered as that of a betrayal. All publicity is good publicity.

Archduke Franz Ferdinand. He may have been fine if it wasn't for his driver taking a wrong turn right into the barrel of Gavrilo Princip. One-star rating for that Uber ride.

Adolf Hitler. He managed to hit the double whammy by being both the assassinated and assassin. If you do find yourself in a bunker with the Soviets closing in on you, probably not a bad idea to consider.

Georgi Markov. While not a leader, he was a prominent Bulgarian dissident who was killed by an umbrella. Yes, you read that right. An assassin poisoned the top of an umbrella with ricin and opened it in front of Markov, he was dead 4 days later. Talk about a rainy day.

You should be getting the point by now. Assassinations are more common than you think. They can be extremely creative, and are often carried out by those closest to you. Can you feel your paranoia tingling? You need to be prepared for the potential – and highly likely – moment when an assassin takes their chance on you. It all starts and ends with control.

CONTROL THE SPACE

You should have a small cadre of bodyguards at this juncture. If you don't, what the hell are you doing? Use them to create a constant buffer zone around you. Whether you are walking around the city, having them run in parallel with your armored limousine, or simply walking to the kitchen to help make you a sandwich, you should always have a six-foot radius created by your bodyguard entourage, plus, this it is good practice for social distancing in this new hellscape we live in.

Control the People

Remember the lesson about rewarding your loyalists? Well you should continue to keep your kiss-asses, sycophants, and die-hard fans happy with bribery. On the other side of the coin, you can use a fair amount of fear (as discussed earlier) to keep them in line. Keep a good balance between the carrot and the stick with your loyalists. They need to be on their toes as much as you need to be on yours when it comes to trust. (Hint: There is none.)

Control the Environment

Bulletproof cars, bulletproof vests, bulletproof windows, planes, and doors. Bulletproof it all. A majority of assassinations are still done in the traditional, gun-in-the-face-now-you're-dead method. For the true paranoia splurge, build a bunker-like dacha in the wilderness to spend most of your time in. Have complicated codes, passwords, and constant changes to security measures. You will certainly be safer, but will you truly be able to live while denying freedoms to others? That is the double-edged sword of dictatorship.

Control the Food

Sometimes an assassin just cannot get the gun to your head. They will often then try getting to your stomach. Ricin, anthrax, various poisons in food, and polonium tea have been useful tactics for assassins in the past and are still in use today. It is good to have several food and beverage tasters at your disposal – and they will be disposed of eventually given your long rule. While that first hot bite of apple pie might be tempting, it is far better to get the second bite and know you will make it to the third bite. Be sure to have tasters with sophisticated palates, they tend to be able to smell something off about your food and thus can cut down on your budget of replacing them. You would be surprised how many tasters you can go through in a month.

BOND, PLENTY OF TIME TO DIE

You cannot forget that as you gain infamy, there will secret British agents knocking at your door. This is especially the case if you are planning greater world domination. If they are as wildly unprofessional as Ian Fleming's famous character, they will announce themselves in the open. This often happens at high stakes baccarat games, exclusive ski chalets, or along the carpeted halls of five-star hotels and chateaus. Most pragmatic scholars of the franchise will simply say, "Shoot him immediately." Not a bad tactic, but where is the flash in that? You have an entire country at your disposal, including its intelligence apparatus. Play some games with him if you can, plus you may get a chance at a Bond girl or two in the process. Just know when to call it a day and actually throw him in the shark tank. It can be tough to end the teasing, but don't worry, James Bond will return.

MOLTO BELLA, CASUS BELLI

On a long enough timeline, your citizens will get antsy, they will get restless, and they will get angry. While the Blame Game is always the first attempt to mitigate damage, it may not be as effective as it was during your campaign and early years in office. This is often because you have removed many of the groups over the years.

In the case of prolonged or rising anger in the populace, the most surefire way to redirect their ire is to look outside your borders. It is time to justify a war! This is also known as "Casus Belli," which in the simplest of terms is to start a war outside your borders to control events inside your borders. The UN Charter specifically prohibits this, which only makes it more fun. You will, however, need to generate a specific "incident" to provide some justification for your aggression. This is akin to a false flag operation, but it must lead to a foreign influence being blamed. You best bet is to utilize some of your forced labor camp workers to help stage the incident – perhaps promise them that their families will be safe, as long as they carry out the mission. Not that they really have a choice in the matter.

There are plenty of great historical examples you can draw on to design your Casus Belli. Hitler managed several dozen small attacks in 1939, including one on a radio station, to help justify his invasion of Poland. The George W. Bush administration invented the idea of Weapons of Mass Destruction (WMDs) to get the public galvanized for the Iraq War in the Middle East. Most recently, Vladimir Putin was able to annex Ukrainian Crimea by fabricating the need to unite the Russian people. He even went so far as to sneak in Russian soldiers without insignia. And for his subsequent war, he claimed Ukraine was full of drug-taking Nazis imposing genocide on their own people. That's some chutzpah.

The point is that there are plenty of creative ways to manufacture consent and justification for your war effort. Some of unused tactics can include:

- "That foreign country canceled our Netflix subscription."
- "That foreign country said that the Lord of the Rings movie franchise was overrated."
- "That foreign country took the last slice of pizza and didn't even pay for it."
- "That foreign country didn't turn off their cell phone in the theater."

Any of these reasons can be manufactured and are more than enough grounds to engage in a fully-fledged war with the foreign country.

You will probably need to sustain the war effort for at least six months before you can start to pull out. People are fickle; they will also get tired of the war. As long as you keep their attention on it long enough, they will move on and forget who or what they were mad about. That will easily buy you another four to five years before you need to deflect again.

Break Glass in Case of Coup

For those of you who went straight to Chapter 7 rather than win power through democratic means, you will already be somewhat familiar with the coup. Well, now you are on the other side of the uprising. Therefore, it is best to prepare for a coup, whether you have experienced organizing one or not.

Militarize the Family

And familiarize the military. An oft-used method for authoritarians is to install family members into key leadership positions in the military. Cousin Ahmed in the Air Force, Aunt Beatrice as Vice-Admiral of the Navy, Grabby Uncle Hank as one of the Joint Chiefs of Staff. This has proven especially effective in the Gulf states, like Iraq, Saudi Arabia, and Syria. The most likely group to organize coups is the military, so by ensuring you have a strong level of oversight and familial ties integrated within the ranks, you stand a better chance of preventing a coup, or stopping it before it gets very far. As you go further down your ranks and potentially run out of family members to install (unless you are Saudi Arabia), be sure to add loyalists of your tribe, ethnicity, softball team, book club, or religion to other parts of your regime.

Fig. 27: Kids Prefer Military Appointments For Their Birthday Presents

It's Your Friend, the CIA

If you decided to work with the CIA for one of your early projects, then congratulations! You have already set up a relationship to help you prevent coups and stomp out emerging opponents. The CIA can – for a price, of course – help infiltrate guerrilla or opponent groups and either assassinate key leaders or provide enough information to crush any insurgency before it becomes a bigger problem. This has been widely used – and successfully – in Latin America. Friends are like a second family, so it is good to rely on them, as long as you get something in return.

Purge to Preserve

If you cannot rely on friends and family, then you will have to rely fully on fear and force. Some days you just need to flush out saboteurs. Try to do it on Fridays like most business leaders. Authoritarians around the world have historically gone through a phase of purging, sometimes early on in their reign after a successful election or coup. Sometimes, years down the road, a subset of angry followers or instigators will have begun to cause enough of a stir to be troublesome. Be proactive here. Nip it in the bud. As soon as you hear any complaints, kill them, send them to a labor camp, and/or threaten their family. It is always best to remove the weed by the root.

Delegate Death

It is important to have a helpful henchman or "number 2" to help carry out the dirty work of these purges mentioned in the above section for you. You need to keep those hands clean. Plenty of henchmen achieved a level of fame close to that of their leader. Adolf Hitler and Heinrich Himmler, Stalin and Genrikh Yagoda – who was killed and replaced by Nikolai Yezhov – who was also then killed and replaced by Beria (Lots of turnover there. They probably should have had more team-building exercises.). Ahmed

Hassan Al-Bakr had Saddam Hussein, who he subsequently over-threw and found his own henchmen. Last but certainly not least, there was George W. Bush and The Android Corpse of Dick Cheney who controlled Bush like a Sesame Street puppet.

Another helpful tool in your purge pocket is the use of death squads controlled solely by you. These groups of trained military killers are useful in carrying out "extrajudicial" (i.e., illegal) executions and other violent acts to maintain your status quo as leader. "Papa Doc" Duvalier of Haiti, who named his death squad after the Haitian Boogeyman, utilized it to quell the opposition and to hold onto power for many years. More recently, Rodrigo Duterte of the Philippines had the Davao Group. They are responsible for killing men, women, and children suspected of petty crime and drug offenses. Just say no, kids. Hell, *Judge Dredd* is widely acclaimed by Hollywood audiences, despite him being a one-man death squad. A few other notable death squads include:

- Squadron of Death (El Salvador)
- Rapid Action Battalion (Bangladesh)
- Beliebers (United States)
- Ustaše (Croatia)
- Kadyrovites (Chechnya)
- Golden Girls (United States)

Lastly, take some advice from Machiavelli, who wrote *The Prince* (he also wrote *Purple Rain*) and be sure to publicly execute your henchman or henchmen after the purge is complete. It is a great way to shift the blame to a "rogue deputy" and keep your hands clean. Happy hunting!

Surviving a Coup

You have managed to brush off the dust from the bomb that exploded under your bed. Thank god for that steel reinforcement. Now you have picked this book up again and need to figure out what is next.

First, you need to look at the previous section and conduct

mass purges across your cabinets, military personnel, and civil servants. It is better to conduct these in public, so break out the firing squads and guillotines in the squares. You need to make an example of who that tried to overthrow you, and fortuitously, those who are caught in the crossfire.

Well, who do you purge? On a spectrum from one to everyone, you need to toggle your guillotine a long way to the right. In an ideal scenario, you will have a solid set of records on all your supporters. Check family first; there is usually one that is involved in some capacity. Things change after all, right? Eliminate them immediately and forget the fanfare. The military is next, if they weren't the major aggressor – and most often, they are – then you will need to look at previous conversations with other members of your government.

Torture time! Be sure to give your intelligence officials a chance to dust off their waterboards and force some confessions out of people, true or not. This is where you can truly test out the strength of your intelligence apparatus: not only with torture, but with its ability to monitor, record, and use that information to blackmail or coerce suspects. So get those officers going as soon as you can, even before the dust settles.

A 2018 study by the aptly named *Journal of Peace Research* concluded that leaders who survive coup attempts and subsequently purge suspected contributors are far more likely to have a long reign than those who just sit on their satin couches and hope for the best. There is no time like the present to ensure the future. Now get your ass up, change into a nice new uniform or pants suit [Chapter 4] and get to removing all those who may have been a part of the coup. And while you are at it, this is a good time to get rid of your useless nephews and nieces. You need to clean house, as they say.

MANDATORY FUN

It is not all doom, gloom, and paranoia in the later years. There is still plenty to enjoy while you hold on tightly to the reins of power. You may end up cowering in a bunker somewhere in the hills at the end, but there is no reason why you cannot spend plenty of time on your yachts and dachas in the interim. Let's end on a high note and talk about some of the luxuries of the later years of authoritarianism.

FIND YOUR CASTLE

Or build it. Isn't it time to upgrade your Presidential Palace? You need to give yourself a large, ostentatious gift for all the hard work you have done holding onto power. Perhaps you could follow the Turkish President, Recep Erdogan, who famously built a palace consisting of 1,150 rooms. Then there is always our dear friend, the well-known pig wrestler Putin, who built a palace so large that it has its own airport.

Columns are obviously a must as a show of extreme wealth. Gold filigree, marble, and statues looking over your Olympic size indoor pool will provide additional garish detail to your palatial home.

Of course, you would be silly to limit yourself to one home. Be sure to buy additional houses across the globe, but be careful, as you don't want to set foot in foreign countries that don't mind following an extradition treaty.

SAIL THE HIGH SEAS

Don't limit yourself and your cadre of sycophants to the land. Every good authoritarian and tech billionaire has a super yacht. You should have your own as well - one that rivals most Carnival cruise lines. No less than two helicopter pads, a 30+ live-in staff, and a state-of-the-art missile defense system are key attributes for your water toy. You can have epic yacht parties with the likes of Jeff Bezos, Roman Abramovich, Jerry Jones, and the Saudi

Crown Prince. Wipe the blood off your dock shoes, turn on the Steve Winwood playlist, and get grooving to the waves of the ocean.

CORONATION

Maybe you have already done this in your initial year as ruler. This is often true if you won via coup and perhaps if you have taken control of a country that still clings to the archaic vestiges of the monarchy. You know who I'm talking about, England.

If not, this could be an official, over-the-top display of wealth that also doubles as a way to elevate you into a god-like figure for your people. Jean-Bedel Bokassa held a grand coronation ceremony when he took power in the Central African Republic. The ceremony cost 20 percent of the total GDP of the country. The buffet tables were extraordinary and the after-party went on for days. You could even have your own Netflix original series one day.

MANHUNTER

An oldie but a goodie. You now have the opportunity to live out the dream of owning an island – probably in the South Pacific Ocean – where you can hunt the most dangerous game of all. Alternatively, perhaps you have the mentality of a mad scientist and would rather go the route of Dr. Moreau. If you want to take a more modern-day approach, create your own *Squid Game*. However, you may want to change the name; those Netflix copyright lawyers are bloodthirsty. Any way you choose, this is also a great way to bring your authoritarian friends over for a bit of fun gamesmanship at the expense of human life.

L'ETAT C'EST MOI

Louis XIV was rumored to have ownership of nearly all the buildings in France, plus he kept ownership of his head unlike his later successor. This principle was known as *L'etat C'est Moi* or "I myself am the nation." Many other authoritarians had a similar claim, such as Rafael Trujillo of the Dominican Republic. You should be well on your way to this if you have successfully nationalized all public services and resources while simultaneously bullying anyone who may have owned key buildings in the past. Of course, if you took the route of selling all your assets to China, then this is probably a no-go.

SPACE TOURISM

Why not reach for the stars? It is easier than ever before; you do not even need any semblance of a space program. There are several insane, narcissistic billionaires who will have no qualms about taking authoritarianism into the stratosphere. Hell, some of them are already planning to have their own slave mines on Mars. You probably have a lot in common with them. There will be plenty to talk about on the ride up to the edge of the atmosphere.

Fig. 28: Come Fly With Me

Should the past have happened?

This historical figure has been temporarily de-statued to foster dialogue about whether different events would have been preferable.

CHAPTER 10

ENSURING YOUR LEGACY

"I want you to know that everything I did, I did for my country."

— POL POT, HISTORY TEACHER

Congratulations, dear leader, you have successfully managed to rise to power, take control, and cling onto it. As you look upon your kingdom amid your twilight years, it is time to complete your final project – solidifying your legacy.

WAR CRIMES: THE HAGUE AND YOU

The International Criminal Court, located at the Hague in the Netherlands, has been trying authoritarians for nearly 20 years. If they haven't already, they are probably going to turn their eye toward you, especially as you reach the later years of your rule. They really are a judgy bunch.

As you recall from Chapter 8, genocide is not recommended. The Hague loves to prosecute these types of petty crimes. Even if you managed to avoid eradicating an entire race or religion of people, there are other crimes that they might target you for. This judicial body in the Netherlands can bring you to court for torture, corporal punishment, mutilation, going to the bathroom without washing your hands, hostage taking, forgetting to wipe your feet before walking into a friend's house, and many more minor indiscretions.

Thankfully, it is incredibly easy to avoid the Hague because, like the United Nations, they are a nearly useless international body without any "teeth." First off, discredit the institution as early as you can in your career as absolute ruler. As discussed earlier, you need to have a consistent campaign to undermine the legitimacy of all international organizations.

Next, tell them to buzz off. You don't have to answer to any of the demands of the Hague. It is not as if they have any army or special forces soldiers who can bring you into their court. The major downside is that you won't be able to leave your country much toward the end of your reign. Also, be careful of extradition treaties at any of your vacation houses in other countries.

BRANDING: SLAP YOUR NAME ON IT

Throughout your reign, you should have been pushing your brand. Marketing is essential to your legacy – during your rule and after you pass into dictator Valhalla. You need to be able to place your name on all buildings regardless.

That new sports stadium, you know the one that hosts your degenerate soccer/football club? That is now named after you. The public library as well as the libraries at the universities also now carry your name. Forget the irony.

If you haven't already, you need to redesign your country's currency with your face on it (the younger version of course – never show age to your citizens) with a ribbon across it saying something like "Fear Before Fanfare." Do NOT use your face on the lower bills or coins though. You do not want to associate yourself with the lower end of the currency spectrum. It is better to have your cheap bills printed with nationalistic symbols or perhaps a historical figure that represents the glory days of your country. You need to be on the bigger bills. Try to use pastel colors for the money too. Your people won't think so much about how little they have when they can appreciate the colorful designs of the few bills they have for food. Either way, given how you have probably run the country, the local currency will be devalued beyond to point of sustainability. Much like the best days of Zimbabwe under Robert Mugabe's reign where $10 million could potentially get you a loaf of bread.

STATUES AND PORTRAITS: A MONUMENTAL LEGACY

Fig. 29: Choose Epic Poses For Your Monuments

There are few better ways to solidify your legacy then building statues of your likeness as well as the major symbols that defined your reign across the country. This is a task you need to assign midway through your career. This is partly because it takes a fair amount of time to sit for various busts, figures, and portraits. You want to be alive to see the majority of your monuments and paintings unveiled to the public. This is also a great excuse to have a party to celebrate all of your accomplishments over the previous decades. There is no reason you shouldn't be able to enjoy your marble obelisks while you are also still occupying your mortal coil.

BRONZE, MARBLE, GOLD

Why not all three? Bronze does well in the outdoors and can be a perfect material for your statues in parks, outside of your stadiums, and in the middle of roundabouts so your citizens can marvel at your figure on their way to their soul-crushing jobs every day – long after you have shed your aforementioned mortal coil. Marble busts are a must in the Olympic swimming pools across town, not just in your palaces. Marble will also do well in the "[Your Name] National Smithsonian Museum." Sure, Smithsonian is an American nuance, but there is no reason you cannot co-opt it for your own selfish needs. And gold? Well, gold works just about everywhere. At your new opera theater, in the terminal at your Airport that all arriving passengers must pass before entering, and at all the government buildings that are still being used for actual governance. It is important that you utilize many statues to show everyone that you will always be watching over them.

FRAME THE FAME

Every U.S. president has his portrait painted and displayed in the White House and at least one museum. You should do the same and even go further. Although it is best to utilize a national artist, if your country is strained in the artistic area, paying top dollar for a famous artist is always a solid choice. But what style do you choose? You most certainly want to commission a more official painting with you sitting or standing regally on or next to an ostentatious chair to show your power and wealth. You may also consider a more traditional fresco that has you pushing back against the evils of communism, socialism, capitalism, democracy, and any other governmental form that attempts to take your power away. A good fresco will have a halo behind your head to accompany your ascension to a godlike state.

Heir Apparent: Siring the Next Generation

Although statues are far easier to create and they don't require 18 years of care, you will absolutely need to create the next generation of children to carry on your name and, more importantly, your rule. You will want to sire one to three children during your first marriage. You will have multiple marriages, but you will want to utilize your first one to develop your heirs. Beyond that, it's mostly just mistresses that you have to bribe to go anywhere near you.

The Son You Never Wanted

All authoritarians want a son to eventually take over their rule and carry on their name. It's genetics, or maybe it's misogyny. Either way, it is supposed to ensure your name lives on outside of an inanimate statue or picture. Unfortunately, your son is probably a totally useless failure. It is fairly common for dictators to sire these types of children. A kid growing up with unlimited money, everything at their fingertips, minions eager not to upset them, and no healthy method to teach them the hardships of life usually turns into a total jerk. For instance, consider all the Trump progeny, or the granddaughter of Benito Mussolini, a right-wing politician (go figure). They are all denser than rocks yet crave the amount of power that their father earned. You should take this section as a red flag to give your spoiled brood a lesson in real life so he doesn't become a completely untethered sociopath. That should occur only after he has taken the throne and earned the undeserved trust of the people. Nepotism is incredibly useful, but if you bring in an unliked son your legacy will end rather quickly. Invest in your future by investing in your son's future – as long as your son's future is about showcasing your past. The Kim Jong family of North Korea has managed this successfully over the last 50 years. Take a page from Kim Jong Il's book and send your son (Kim Jon Un) to a fancy boarding school in Switzerland. Get him familiar with the intricacies of Western monarchy, capitalism, and oligarchy so he can bring it back to your country and live it each day.

The Daughter, the Queen

Your son is a complete idiot. You sent him to school, and this first-born is a major failure. Perhaps you name him after yourself so you can use him as a scapegoat if the criminal prosecutors come knocking (e.g., Donald Trump Jr.). Your daughter on the other hand, is the apple of your eye. She is an example of pure innocence to the people and dulls the edges of your sharp reign. Market her early and often. Your citizens will love seeing her on camera and staged photos and videos of you playing with her will soften your image and improve your overall legacy.

There have been plenty of daughters of former authoritarians who went on to live normal lives. Apart from the daughter of Mussolini, the daughter of the dictator Efrain Rios Montt of Guatemala (who took over the country in 1982) has become prominent in the United States. She married Republican congressman Jerry Weller in 2004. There is no doubt they had plenty of pillow talk about with regard to authoritarianism.

However, let's not forget there are plenty of daughters who end up being hated by the populace. This could be detrimental for your legacy. For example, Gulnara Karimova, the daughter of former Uzbekistan president, Islam Karimov (he died in 2016) was known as the "single most hated person" in the country. Somehow she was fairly prolific in her career, as she became known as a Screenplay Writer (she probably wrote *The Emoji Movie*), a University Professor, Fashion Designer, Telecom Magnate, and Obsessive Twitter User. Let's just say she has had plenty of delusions of grandeur.

Another good example is the former dictator of Angola, Isabel dos Santos, who also brings a breath of equality to our tally of dictators. She took over from her father in 2016. Her reign lasted a measly one year, but she managed to pilfer the country's resources to the tune of $2 billion. Not a bad annual salary. She certainly tarnished her family's name in Angola, and remains under corruption investigation. She will probably never face any charges and live on a yacht in the Seychelles. Isn't justice fun?

YOUR NAME FOREVER

Regardless of whether you have a failure of a son or a promising young woman of a daughter, you need to get your name integrated into theirs as another way of ensuring your legacy. For sons, it's fairly easy. Name them the same as you and just slap a "Jr." or an "II" at the end. Last names last, but first names last longer. Your daughter will have her own name, although you can try to just add an "a" after yours for her name too. Sure, "Stalina" might be strange at first, but your citizens will be quick to adopt it and love it. Otherwise, they will be sent to the Stalina camps. Hell, you can name your kid "I Hate You" and you will still get him or her to rule the country with no troubles. It is good to be the king and also good to be the child of a king.

PASSIONS AND PECULIARITIES

Developing your crazy passions and peculiarities is one of the most fun activities you can engage in over your reign. This is something you need to start to germinate in your early years, which will become a binding characteristic and eventually a major distinction in your legacy years. So start practicing your narcissistic lying technique as early as possible.

UNBELIEVABLE ACHIEVEMENTS

In your multiple decades of rule, you accomplished a lot for your country. You succeeded in even greater ways for yourself. If you haven't already, it is time to broadcast what you have achieved in your divine rule – regardless of its authenticity.

Sports

It is amazing how well you play golf. Think of Kim Jong Il, who was able to bag a hole-in-one across 18 holes; you can do the same. In fact, you can do better. That Par Three course? Well you just shot a zero on it; somehow, you managed to get the ball in the hole without even swinging your club. That is impressive. How about soccer? It was amazing to see you score 30 goals in the first half of the game against Manchester United. Sure, the Manchester United team didn't seem to have their key players, they were wearing neon green jerseys, which said "Monchoster Blunited," and three of their players were executed before the half started, but you won fair and square.

The Arts

That Jackson Pollock-like crayon drawing that you did while drunk on $15,000 whiskey is a triumph of the modern art scene. Your citizens applaud it as it is displayed on state television across the country. It will be shown at all the museums and appreciated by the fussiest of art critics. It does not matter how many war crimes you may have committed. Once you started painting, no matter how terrible your skills are, you will somehow be forgiven for all transgressions. Look at George W. Bush, he started two wars, drained the coffers of his country and is now seen as a sensitive artist. As we have noted, people are daft and have the attention span of a lab rat, so you should have no trouble plastering over any war crimes, famines, or other issues by simply painting a mediocre picture for the fans and the news.

Beyond the Body – Manifest Fun

You cannot possibly move into the afterlife without showcasing your skills and talents in random areas of human achievement. Kim Jong Il – as the myth goes – never pooped in his life. So why not take it a step further? Not only did you never poop because your body is 100 percent efficient, but you were able to transcend the ordinary lot of humanity out of nothing more than your efficiency. Your kneecaps are amazing and as silly as that sounds, it works. It is surprising how many idiots will worship random body parts of you. Get them out there and win the crowd.

THE TOUCH OF GOD

If you managed to fund a coronation, then you are already a step ahead. Every dictator worth their body weight in gold eventually develops a god complex. In fact, in North Korea, Kim Il-Sung still remains their "eternal president" even though he has been dead for 30 years. Now that is a legacy! There is no reason you should stray from this path. You are touched by the almighty, in fact, you are the almighty. It is imperative that you push out this narrative as soon as you can to cement your legacy for hundreds of years. The only thing better than a living god is a dead one because a dead god can do no wrong. Even better, your mythos will grow long after you have passed on to the afterlife. This is a fairly common phenomenon among authoritarians who have passed on. Often, you will gain new traits that you didn't even think of when you were living. It is easier for your loyalists and heirs to create these new traits when you have established yourself as a deity. The lord works in mysterious ways, after all.

YOUR MAUSOLEUM – GET AHEAD OF THE DEAD

Like the great pharaohs of the past, you require a tomb that requires thousands of man-hours and hundreds of kilos of stone. There are many great mausoleum designs to choose from today, so you don't have to settle for a boring 3D triangle. With the technology today, you can project your likeness on a 100-foot wall for all of eternity. Or at least until your country collapses in on itself due to in-fighting.

You should also consider having your body embalmed and displayed for all your supporters to admire long after you have died. For decades, Vladimir Lenin continues to be displayed for all to see in Moscow. You may want to even go further than just lying-in state and have yourself suspended in mid-air over the central square of the capital city, continuously lording it over your people even when the light in your eyes has long since gone out.

Conclusion

Good Night and Gulag!

"It is not truth that matters but victory."

— Adolf Hitler, Chocolate Lover

The time has come to close the curtains on your rule. Alas, all authoritarian reigns must come to an end, despite many attempts at immortality. If you followed this book, then your rule should be long, prosperous, and infamous. You have claimed victory for decades, avoided attempts at being overthrown, and cemented your legacy. There are only a few remaining loose ends to tie up as you close your eyes for the final time on your empire.

Death Before Exile

You're not my homeland anymore
So what am I defending now?

These lyrics by Taylor Swift better define exile than any tweed-wearing historian. If you do find yourself ripped from your homeland due to a coup or attempted assassination, or to escape justice, or avoid your in-laws visiting for the holidays, be sure to include these lyrics in your speeches to your people from afar.

If you managed to successfully follow the tactics in Chapter 9, you will hopefully never have to choose between death and exile. If you do find yourself having to spend your final days in exile, do not despair. You are in great company with the likes of Napoleon Bonaparte on Saint Helena or Elba, Wilhelm II of Germany in the Netherlands, Donald Trump in Mar-A-Lago, and Mos Def in South Africa.

Exile need not mean the end. Just look at the scrappy history of Napoleon, who managed to escape his island prison and conquer France all over again. He was like a bad ex-girlfriend or boyfriend that France just couldn't say no to; it must have been his animal magnetism. If you have maintained a set of loyalists in your country, there is always the possibility of sneaking you back into your country on the tails of a countercoup. Never give up; that is what got you here after all, right?

If you decide to live out your days in exile, this is a good time to take up some hobbies to keep you busy. Consider taking up macrame, knitting, or writing your autobiography. Of course, you won't actually be writing it. All writers are losers so they're cheap to hire.

Your Struggle – A Memoir

Nearly every authoritarian manages to publish an autobiography in their lifetime or at the very least to have someone write it for them. You should ensure your memoir is published before you are dead; this will help further cement your legacy and legend.

Be sure to start your biography off with how you dealt with and eventually overcame the struggles in your early life – a parent's death, war and strife, or that you couldn't buy the Play-Station 5 when it was first released. It was these struggles, and how you overcame them, that defined who you have become today. Feel free to pull out the buzz phrases from your campaign trail for chapter titles; just dust off the old hits [see also Chapter 5].

You should never actually put pen to paper either. Dictate your words. Dictating is always the right choice. Hire an experienced ghostwriter to fluff up your accomplishments, your struggles, and your love of the country.

Finally, title your book something that requires a colon – much like many of the sub-sections of this book. A few examples:

[Your Name]: A Life in Power
[Your Name]: Long Walk to Oppression
[Your Name]: The Diary of a Young Girl
[Your Name]: I Know Why the Caged Bird Sings (Because I Put It There)
[Your Name]: Becoming

Good luck as you encapsulate your life on the written page. It is a shame that most of your citizens cannot read. That wasn't because you defunded public education, though. No, no, definitely something else.

⊕ ✠ ⚡ 卐 ☭

Your Final Parade

It is time to plan your final march down your own Red Square. Alas, you will not be alive to see it, but you can certainly plan all its fanfare beforehand. Your final send-off must be one that all will remember for generations.

Military Escort

Regardless of whether you came from the military or ascended into power through the civilian route, a ceremonial parade isn't as powerful without a military escort. Soldiers marching in goose-step unison, fighter jets being towed as a showcase, rows and rows of rocket-launching trucks and tanks, and a marching band. Who doesn't love a marching band? Some great examples to pull ideas from are the Moscow Victory Parade of 1945, celebrating the defeat of Nazi Germany, or perhaps China's Military Parade in 2019 for the 70th anniversary of the founding of communist China. It is important to display your country's military strength despite your lack of being alive.

Giant Portraits

The people need to see you and remember you at your most glorious. You should have commissioned multiple portraits over your reign: a copy of these can be made as a showcase. Take a page from North Korea's rulebook and put them on jeeps or trucks, surrounded by flowers to be driven slowly down the promenade. You should expect to have your citizens bow at the site of each portrait, gnash their teeth, and display inordinate amounts of grief. At least ensure that you have previously installed loyalists among the crowd to do so and that the military police have been briefed to watch out for any insufficiently heartbroken behavior.

Fig. 30: Portraits For Your Final Parade

Macy's Floats and Balloons

What is a parade without floats of beloved television and movie characters? You need to have various floats and balloons to entertain the people. The Pillsbury Doughboy played an important role at the funeral for Kim Jong-Il... or maybe that was Kim Jong Un. Baby Yoda is a big hit these days, so be sure to get that balloon out in your parade; kids and adults will love it. And of course, everyone loves Snoopy, a Charles Schulz classic for decades who will fit well in any parade – feel free to draw a military uniform on him.

Goodbye Dear Leader

Our time has run out. Despite many attempts by scientists, humanity has failed to solve death yet, although major improvements to the chalupa have taken their attention away.

If you successfully followed the advice of this guide, you should have managed to conquer your country, oppress your people, and sustain your rule. A rich life indeed. Don't be sad that it is over; be angry that you cannot live forever until the heat death of the universe. Be happy that it happened. You are in rarefied air, in the company of a small handful of leaders who were praised, feared, and adored. May your memory be etched in the stones of time for all eternity, on top of the mass graves of your detractors. Goodnight, sweet prince.

Appendix

The Great Pioneers of Despotism

There are plenty of great leaders who have decorated the annals of authoritarianism. The following pages list some of the best known – as well as some of the lesser-known examples. Never be afraid to steal characteristics, ideas, and hobbies from them. They would appreciate it and do the same to you if they could.

The list below is non-exhaustive, but it contains many of the insane innovators, deranged despots, and mentally ill men of strength. These are the pioneers who paved the way, leaving in their wake bodies, destruction, and opportunities for future dictators like yourself.

.

JOSEF STALIN

Assumed Power: April 1922
Country: Soviet Union
Length of Terror: 31 Years
Cause of Death: Really Bad Headache
Interests: Camp Counselor, People Person, Loves Winter
Favorite Food: Gulag Goulash, Served Cold
Favorite Pokémon: Raticate

With an infectious laugh, Good Old Uncle Joe helped change the USSR from a country of serfs into a country of serfs that worked in industrialized factories. He loved to sit on his dacha and watch the Germans fail to win Stalingrad while sending wave after wave of his countrymen to their deaths.

ADOLF HITLER

Assumed Power: January 30, 1933
Country: Germany
Length of Terror: 12 Years
Cause of Death: Adolf Hitler
Interests: Meth Addict, Dog Lover, Volunteered at the Suicide Prevention Hotline
Favorite Food: Swastika Strudel
Favorite Pastime: Watching Fox News

An avid painter, Adolf, or "A-Dog" as he was known by nobody, loved to walk around his fortified castle in the Bavarian Alps. He was proactive in wanting to help other European countries by invading them. His favorite books were charred ones.

Nicolae Ceausescu

Assumed Power: 1965
Country: Romania
Length of Terror: 24 years
Cause of Death: A Bullet to the Face
Interests: Diabetic, Fashionista, Haircuts
Favorite Food: Lasagna
Favorite Shoe Brand: Air Jordans

A fashion guru with a pompadour haircut, despite his communist party leanings. He managed to acquire a healthy number of clothes, shoes, and hats along with his wife, Elena. He oversaw a mass surveillance apparatus, repression, and rationing of necessities. His people managed to save up for a few bullets for him and his wife.

Donald Trump

Assumed Power: January 20, 2017
Country: United States of America
Length of Terror: 4 Years
Cause of Death: Sadly, He Remains Alive
Interests: Steaks, Vodka, Gambling
Favorite Food: Niçoise Salad
Favorite Trump: Himself

A rancid turd that was brought to life from true love's kiss, Donald struggled to be successful, as he had to rely on his wits and a $1 million loan from his father. He has been successful in bankrupting multiple casinos and businesses. He remains a dictator-in-exile.

SHEEV PALPATINE

Assumed Power: 84 BBY (Before the Battle of Yavin)
Galaxy: A Far, Far Away One
Length of Terror: 157 Years
Cause of Death: Suicide, Twice
Interests: Electricity, Cloaks, Senate Rules
Favorite Food: Roasted Porg
Favorite Movie Franchise: *The Bourne Supremacy*

Also known as Darth Sidious, he took advantage of bureaucratic fundamentals to manipulate people and eventually take over an entire galaxy. Palpatine managed to live through nine movies before succumbing to the screenwriters. During his life, he killed many species across the galaxy. He is survived by whomever Disney can productize next.

ROBERT MUGABE

Assumed Power: December 31, 1987
Country: Zimbabwe
Length of Terror: 31 Years
Cause of Death: Bitterness
Interests: Economics Professor, British Colonialism Lover,
Cricket Fan
Favorite Food: Elephant Meat
Favorite Currency: Monopoly Money

F ollowing a similar trajectory to Nelson Mandela, Mugabe
was imprisoned for a decade before unleashing his revenge
on white people – and then eventually on black people
too, in the name of equality. A high level of repression coupled
with the highest level of inflation ever recorded kept him in power
until his early 90s.

Mohammad Bin Salman

Assumed Power: January 23, 2015
Country: Kingdom of Saudi Arabia
Length of Terror: Ongoing
Cause of Death: N/A
Interests: Woodworking, U.S. Missile Collector, Yachts, Human Rights Advocate
Favorite Food: Beef Bacon
Favorite Hand Tool: Bone Saw

Although still considered a Crown Prince, Bin Salman has been the power behind the throne for several years. A lover of repression, particularly through social media, he has attempted to remove anyone who even stands next to a critic of the regime. One claim to fame is exploiting WhatsApp to hack Jeff Bezo's phone – not a good way to get yourself into space anytime soon.

BENITO MUSSOLINI

Assumed Power: March 23, 1919
Country: Italy
Length of Terror: 25 Years
Cause of Death: Gunshot
Interests: Violin, Romance Novels, Aggressive Hand Gestures, Teaching
Favorite Food: Campbell's SpaghettiOs
Favorite Super Mario Brother: Luigi

Considered a pioneer of modern fascism, he helped standardize an entire country that had been fragmented by separate dialects and cultures. Although he took power without a traditional coup, he managed to secure socialist support for a non-socialist end game. While he began with a teaching degree, he quickly realized how badly paid it was and went on to be an absolute ruler.

SAURON

Assumed Power: Second Age (SA) 1500
Country: Mordor
Length of Terror: 1,000 Years
Cause of Death: A Couple Of Little People
Interests: Peeping Tom, Micromanager, Goth Music
Favorite Food: Lembas Bread
Favorite Jewelry: Tiara

A skilled forger, after Sauron finished trade school in welding, he rose up the ranks and eventually took over Mordor. There he tried to bridge the divide between elves, dwarves, and men through his forging skills. Unfortunately, it didn't work.

Kim Jong Il

Assumed Power: July 8, 1994
Country: North Korea
Length of Terror: 17 Years
Cause of Death: Ascended
Interests: Film Buff, Golf Pro, Non-Pooper
Favorite Food: Shark Fin Soup
Favorite Korea: North

B orn on the highest peak of Korea and preceded by a double rainbow, all great and powerful Jong-Il would lead his nation through famine – which he caused – and the threat of nuclear annihilation – which he also caused. He would go toe-to-toe with many leaders throughout his career and did it in the fanciest of pants suits.

Muammar Gaddafi

Assumed Power: September 1, 1969
Country: Libya
Length of Terror: 42 Years
Cause of Death: Friendly Fire
Interests: Crushed On Condoleezza Rice, Virgin Bodyguards, Bunga Bunga Parties
Favorite Food: Camel Meat
Favorite Position: Missionary

Born in a tent and from a nomadic family, Gaddafi would rise up in the country through his military service. He seized control through a military coup and would eventually rule over four decades of harsh repression, funding of terrorism and other radical groups (e.g., IRA, Black Panthers, Nation of Islam).

MAO ZEDONG

Assumed Power: March 20, 1943
Country: People's Republic of China
Length of Terror: 33 Years
Cause of Death: Back-to-Back Heart Attacks
Interests: Pants Suits, Concubines, the Free Market
Favorite Food: General Tso's Chicken
Favorite President: Richard Nixon

Mao led his country's communist revolution, which helped him become its de facto leader. He would go on to oversee the worst famines in history making such brilliant decisions as killing all the birds, which led to locusts eating all the crops. As a true communist, he would be the face of all the nation's currency up to the present day.

Francois "Papa Doc" Duvalier

Assumed Power: October 27, 1957
Country: Haiti
Length of Terror: 14 Years
Cause of Death: Diabetes
Interests: Dressed Like Baron Samedi, Changed "The Lord's Prayer" To Include Himself, Killed All Black Dogs
Favorite Food: Double Bacon Cheeseburger
Favorite God: Himself

D uvalier went to medical school and rose up the ranks as a physician. Using his advanced medical degree, he embraced voodoo mysticism. He organized groups to terrorize his opponents and detractors, before peacefully transferring power to his son, "Baby Doc."

Francisco Macias Nguema

Assumed Power: October 12, 1968
Country: Equatorial Guinea
Length of Terror: 11 Years
Cause of Death: Firing Squad
Interests: Hallucinogenic Drugs, Thought Hitler Was "Savior Of Africa," Banning Eyeglasses
Favorite Food: Anything with CBD
Favorite Dictator: Adolf Hitler

C ame to power when his country gained independence from Spain. He is often considered one of the most brutal dictators in history despite a kill count of only 80,000. He was incredibly anti-European and aligned with the Eastern bloc during the Cold War. His paranoia was such that he banned anything resembling intelligence, including the word "intellectual."

SAPARMURAT NIYAZOV

Assumed Power: November 2, 1990
Country: Turkmenistan
Length of Terror: 16 Years
Cause of Death: Turkmenattack
Interests: Illiterate, Outlawing Lip Synching, Launching Books Into Space
Favorite Food: Gurbansoltanedzhe
Favorite Month: Turkmenbashi

Took over following a coup shortly before breakup of the USSR. He enjoyed a healthy cult of personality that he would extend to renaming everything from foods to the months and days of the week. Was successful in funneling billions into his own coffers and outside of the country, surviving coups to die when his own fat heart gave out.

King Jaffe Joffer

Assumed Power: January 1971
Country: Zamuda
Length of Terror: 30 Years
Cause of Death: The Sequel
Interests: Arranging Marriages, Wearing Animal Skins, Hot Tubbing
Favorite Food: McDowell's Fast Food
Favorite Director: John Landis

Claimed power following a coup and having served in the military. King Jaffe would lead as a benevolent ruler – although one that would make his citizens dance for him. He would eventually invest in a McDonalds-like franchise to further extend his wealth before abdicating to his son on his deathbed.

JUAN PERON

Assumed Power: June 1946
Country: Argentina
Length of Terror: 28 Years
Cause of Death: Love
Interests: Big Hats, Unions, Fencing
Favorite Food: Arby's Waffle Fries
Favorite Wife: Eva Peron

As the generalissimo, Juan helped organize a coup to overthrow President Ramon Castillo. He eventually became leader following the end of World War II. He used popular support to help him win karaoke contests. He also enacted domestic policies that would give him ultimate control.

Ferdinand Marcos

Assumed Power: December 30, 1965
Country: Philippines
Length of Terror: 23 Years
Cause of Death: His Organs Protested
Interests: The "Thrilla in Manila," Lying, Martial Law
Favorite Food: Kare Kare
Favorite Watch: *Omega 12*

Rose to power after hiring an assassin to kill his opponent while he was brushing his teeth. He received ROTC training from the United States to fight in World War II. A trained lawyer, Marcos moved up the ranks in government to eventually become president. He paid lip service to the military to consolidate power in the country for the next quarter of a century.

KIM JONG UN

Assumed Power: December 24, 2011
Country: North Korea
Length of Terror: 11 Years and Counting
Cause of Death: Future Heart Attack
Interests: Intercontinental Ballistic Missiles (ICBMs), Cheese, More Cheese
Favorite Food: Anything with calories
Favorite Haircut: "The Pants Suit"

Having studied in a private school in Switzerland (check out the photo with his dumb blonde hair), he eventually returns to his homeland and takes over from his father, Kim Jong-Il. Over the last decade, he has become fatter and crazier, utilizing the age-old North Korean tactic of threatening nuclear war while starving the majority of his population.

Vladimir Putin

Assumed Power: December 31, 1999
Country: Russia
Length of Terror: 23 Years and Counting
Cause of Death: Hopefully Soon
Interests: Nuclear War, Cold War, *Star Wars*
Favorite Food: Borscht
Favorite Tea: Polonium Blend

Became acting president of Russia after the famous drunk, Boris Yeltsin, ceded the position to him. A high-level KGB agent and mayor, Putin loves long walks in the park that result in the assassination of perceived enemies. He has a desire to revert the world back to the Cold War but uses new age tactics such as malware, disinformation, and Donald Trump to achieve it. Total Asshole.

ALEXANDER LUKASHENKO

Assumed Power: July 20, 1994
Country: Belarus
Length of Terror: 28 Years and Counting
Cause of Death: Likely Balding
Interests: Big Hats, Mustaches, Kowtowing
Favorite Food: Whatever Putin Likes
Favorite Putin: Vladimir

Rose to power following the dissolution of the USSR. Has the claim as longest running president in Europe – although "president" is a misnomer. Claims to be the "last dictator" of Europe, so which is it? He continues to have a stranglehold on his country while being a puppet of Vladimir Putin. Instituted the Russian language as the main language (replacing Belarusian).

GURBANGULY BERDIMUHAMEDOV

Assumed Power: February 14, 2007
Country: Turkmenistan
Length of Terror: 15 Years
Cause of Death: Coupbanguly
Interests: Dentistry, Spinning Hot Beats, Russian Nurses As
Mistresses
Favorite Food: Gold Bars
Favorite Month: Gurbansoltan

Often considered the illegitimate son of the former president, Saparmurat Niyazov. He studied dentistry and was eventually appointed as Minister of Health before taking over from his "father." This was despite having no real qualifications for any type of leadership or politics. Despite optimistic rumors of his death, he remains alive for now.

Idi Amin

Assumed Power: January 25, 1971
Country: Uganda
Length of Terror: 8 Years
Cause of Death/Downfall: Living in Saudi Arabia
Interests: Heavyweight Boxing, Cannibalism, Hitler
Favorite Food: Oranges, So Many Damn Oranges
Favorite Actor: Forest Whitaker

Rose in the ranks of the Uganda military after the country gained independence from Britain in the early 1960s. When the previous leader tried to investigate his actions, he overthrew him with a coup. He became the most brutal African dictator of the century (estimates of 500,000 killed), eventually being forced into exile in Saudi Arabia, and feasting on fast food until he died in 2003.

Nicolas Maduro

Assumed Power: March 5, 2013
Country: Venezuela
Length of Terror: 9 Years And Counting
Cause of Death/Downfall: The Economy
Interests: "Chavismo," Sashes, Just For Men Hair Dye
Favorite Food: "Salt Bae" Steak
Favorite Oil: Beard and Crude

G rew up as your typical middle-class Venezuelan before getting into politics. Won a special election to serve out the term of Hugo Chavez after his death. Showcased himself as a "man of the people," but has quickly tanked the economy, made friends with other dictators, and kept power by blaming the West for his country's ills.

OMAR AL-BASHIR

Assumed Power: October 16, 1993
Country: Sudan
Length of Terror: 26 Years
Cause of Death/Downfall: Military Coup and Irony
Interests: Subdividing Countries, Famine, Genocide
Favorite Food: Starvation
Favorite Facial Expression: Scowl

Grew up in poverty before joining the Egyptian military to fight Israel in the 1970s. Rose quickly through the Sudanese military before leading a coup in the late 1980s. He dissolved the government and became absolute ruler four years later, focusing on Islamic (Sharia) law. A couple of decades, a few famines (Darfur), a genocide, a partition of Sudan into two countries, and a coup later, he was later ousted from rule for good.

CITATIONS

1. Rejoice! Democracy is Dead

1. What did I just say?

Recommended Reading

Hitler, Adolf, *Mein Kampf*
Stalin, Joseph, *The Foundations of Leninism*
Mussolini, Benito, *My Life*
Zedong, Mao, *The Little Red Book*
Gaddafi, Muammar, *The Green Book*
Malice, Michael, *Dear Reader: The Authorized Biography of Kim Jong Il*
Szablowski, Witold, *How to Feed a Dictator*
Carle, Eric, *The Very Hungry Caterpillar*

Also by C. T. Jackson

Leadership Guides

So You Want To Be A Capitalist
So You Want To Be A Monarch
So You Want To Be An NFL Owner
So You Want To Be A Geisha
So You Want To Be A Failed Author

Other Literary Works

Moby Dictator
War and ~~Peace~~ More War
Charlotte's Web of Lies

MEET THE AUTHOR

C.T. Jackson is persona non grata in over 30 countries. He has a total of $52,000 worth of bounties on his head. Mr. Jackson is currently being held in an undisclosed black site somewhere in Eastern Europe with no timetable for release. When he is not being detained by various intelligence authorities, he spends his time with his wife outside of Washington D.C.

ACKNOWLEDGMENTS

This book was a labor camp of love. It would not have been possible without the support of my family, friends, and those I stole from.

To my wife, Melody Ain, dictator of my heart, who supported me through the late nights, bad jokes, and ensuring I only offended the right people.

To my mother, dictator of my childhood, who instilled in me a love of writing and politics that I have used for this silly purpose.

To my cronies, Alex Boeckler, Andrew Carlson, Austin Doyle, Daniel Steiman, Micah Loudermilk, and Matthew Padgett. Without their early thoughts this book would be a total mess.

To Hugh Barker, whose edits tightened the writing to become truly professional. And to Paul Hawkins, whose illustrations brought the words to life and whose advice helped me through this first journey.

Finally, to you dear reader. Sometimes the best way to counter a dictator is to point and laugh at them. Keep pointing and laughing, my friends.

Made in the USA
Middletown, DE
23 October 2022

13310183R00118